CYPRUS AND UGARIT

CYPRUS AND UGARIT

Connecting Material and Mercantile Worlds

A. BERNARD KNAPP

Dedication:
For Cyprus, the island that inspired, nourished and sustained my life in archaeology.

© 2024 A. Bernard Knapp

This book is published under a Creative Commons Attribution-NonCommercial-NoDerivatives 4.0 International License (CC BY-NC-ND 4.0). This license does not apply to content that is attributed to sources other than the copyright holder mentioned above. Under this license you are free to share this work, provided the makers are attributed. Its content cannot be used for commercial purposes nor is it allowed to make adaptations without permission from the copyright holder.

For more information about our licenses, please visit https://www.sidestone.com/publishing/creative-commons.

Published by Sidestone Press, Leiden
www.sidestone.com

Lay-out & cover design: Sidestone Press
Photograph cover:
    The site of Ugarit (photo: Gianfranco Gazzetti, Wikicommons CC BY-SA).
    Copper oxhide ingot (Image courtesy of The Metropolitan Museum of Art).

ISBN 978-94-6426-304-6 (softcover)
ISBN 978-94-6426-305-3 (hardcover)
ISBN 978-94-6426-306-0 (PDF e-book)

DOI: 10.59641/g5j1d2e3f4

Contents

ABSTRACT	9
PREFACE AND ACKNOWLEDGEMENTS	11
1. INTRODUCTION	13
2. BACKGROUND	15
Ugarit	18
Cyprus	23
3. UGARIT AND CYPRUS: COMMON MATERIAL FEATURES	27
Ashlar Masonry	27
Urban Mortuary Practices	29
Composite Anchors	31
Cypro-Minoan Script	33
4. CYPRIOT MATERIAL IN UGARIT	35
Seals and Seal Impressions	36
Metals	37
Pottery	39
5. LEVANTINE MATERIAL IN CYPRUS	47
Levantine Pottery on Cyprus	49
Other Levantine Material on Cyprus	54
6. CYPRUS AND UGARIT: DOCUMENTARY EVIDENCE	57
People, Politics and Professions	57
People	57
Politics	61
Professions	63
7. MATERIAL AND MERCANTILE CONNECTIVITY IN THE LATE BRONZE AGE EASTERN MEDITERRANEAN	65
The Merchants of Ugarit and Cyprus	66
Maritime Sphere(s) of Interaction	71
Mercantile Worlds: Agents and Actors	73
CONCLUSIONS	77
REFERENCES	79
INDEX	109

Abstract

This study examines the detailed archaeological and documentary records of Cyprus and Ugarit (and the wider Levant to the extent feasible) to gain new insights into the long-term relations between two of the best known, well-connected polities in the Late Bronze Age eastern Mediterranean. In so doing, I engage interpretative concepts such as actors and agents, merchants and mercantilism, and maritime spheres (regions) of interaction. Having presented some background on both Ugarit and Cyprus, I consider the common material features of both (e.g., ashlar masonry, urban mortuary practices, composite anchors, the Cypro-Minoan script), and then examine more specifically Cypriot material uncovered in Ugarit (especially seals, metals and pottery), followed by Levantine material found on Cyprus. I then present all the known documentary evidence related to these two polities and discuss this evidence with respect to three factors: people, politics and professions. In the following discussion section, I look more broadly at material and mercantile connectivity in the Late Bronze Age eastern Mediterranean, considering in turn the merchants of Ugarit and Cyprus, maritime spheres of interaction, and the actors and agents involved in these mercantile worlds. In conclusion, I argue that although Ugarit and Cyprus were two very different kinds of society, they shared a vital, commercial link, one that — over time — had a transformative impact on Cyprus.

Preface and Acknowledgements

From the time I wrote my M.A. thesis (Knapp 1973) and published my first major article (Knapp 1983), I have been interested in the long-term relations between Cyprus and Ugarit, two of the best-known polities in the Late Bronze Age eastern Mediterranean. Although I touched upon this topic in other papers (e.g., Knapp 1991, 1993, 1994, 1998; Knapp and Meyer 2023), the daunting amount of material published (or not published, in the case of Ugarit) always gave me reason to pause before confronting it. Even now, after nearly two years of on-again, off-again research and writing this study, in many aspects it remains incomplete, but at least offers a starting point for further research.

Beyond the cultural homogeneity that seems materially evident between Late Bronze Age Cyprus and Ugarit (as well as other northern Levantine coastal sites), economically the two polities were quite distinct. Ugarit was a long-established commercial hub with at least two major ports where all kind of goods — including raw materials — were available. By contrast, Cyprus was a newcomer to the eastern Mediterranean commercial sphere, its main resource being copper, an essential material component of the Bronze Age. Over the course of the Late Bronze Age, the power dynamic between these two polities oscillated and changed dramatically; in this volume I seek to present not only the story of Cyprus *and* Ugarit but also the story of Cyprus *versus* Ugarit.

In the course of writing this work, I have become indebted to several scholars, both for reading and commenting on the text (or parts of it), and for help with the references and illustrations.

For the last, I am especially grateful to Nathan Meyer for preparing Table 1, Figures 6a and 6b (maps) and Figure 9 (plan of Maa *Palaeokastro*). I thank Philip J. Boyes for permission to reproduce here Figure 1 (map of the town at Ugarit) and Figure 2 (map of the kingdom of Ugarit). I also extend my thanks to Giorgios Georgiou, Director of the Cypriot Department of Antiquities, for providing the image of the Canaanite Jar from Arpera *Mosphilos* (Figure 8) and the permission to publish it.

Once again, I extend my deepest thanks to Nathan Meyer for his detailed comments on various iterations of the text. At more than one point in the paper, several key ideas are referenced by a 'personal communication' with him. I am also grateful to Caroline Sauvage for reading and commenting on the text; her expertise on the material and documentary records of Ugarit made her an essential reader. Chris Monroe likewise carefully read the entire text, provided several comments and crucial references, and gave it his *imprimatur*. Equally, I thank Artemis Georgiou, from her Cypriot perspective, for reading and commenting on the full text, and offering more detailed views on the section *Levantine Pottery on Cyprus*. Cassandra Donnelly's close reading and detailed comments (providing multiple references) on the section *Cypro-Minoan Script* ensured that it was up-to-date and (hopefully) free of errors. To all these colleagues, who gave so freely of their own valuable time, I am truly indebted.

Finally, my thanks to Ayla Çevik for preparing the Index.

CHAPTER 1

INTRODUCTION

Writing some 50 years ago in the *Cambridge Ancient History*, Hector Catling (1975: 197) had little to say about relations between Cyprus and Ugarit during the Late Bronze Age (LBA): "The Cypriots continued to enjoy and develop their trade links with the Levant and Egypt throughout L.C. [Late Cypriot] I … Cyprus was free to traffic with North Syria, where Alalakh and Ugarit received a high proportion of the trade." Subsequent fieldwork and research, as well as the publication of earlier excavations at Ugarit, made it possible for Yon (1999a, 2013) to write specifically on relations between Ugarit and Cyprus during the LBA (see the following section). Buchholz (1999) presented a more detailed treatment of material relations between Cyprus and Ugarit, whilst Dietrich (2000) sketched out the textual evidence, both incorporating the Aegean for good measure. By 2021, Bretschneider et al. were able to publish a long paper revolving around Ugarit and a single Cypriot site (Pyla *Kokkinokremos*) at the end of the LBA. In that paper, the authors focused on the 'twilight of the Bronze Age' and observed that "[s]ome questions such as who founded the settlement [Pyla] at this specific, strategic location and why it was abandoned suddenly relatively soon afterwards, cannot be answered definitely but remain important to understand the relationship between Cyprus and Ugarit" (Bretschneider et al. 2021: 608).

With few exceptions (Sauvage 2012; Steel 2013: 29–32), the works just cited and a multitude of others (including excavation reports) that consider Cypro-Levantine relations — be they maritime, economic, iconographic or textual — tend to be traditional material or stylistic analyses, straightforward documentary or philological interpretations (to the extent that documents written in the Ugaritic language and script allow), or singularly focused, science-based analyses (especially of pottery and metals). The stories created by much of this work view relations between Cyprus and Ugarit primarily through the lens of the textual evidence, with its many and diverse references to the merchants of Ugarit and their mercantile practices (most importantly Monroe 2009, 2015; Pardee 2023).

These observations are not intended as criticism of this cornucopia of research output, as it forms the basis for any attempt at a broader, interpretative essay, which is what I seek to present in this study. Taking into account the detailed archaeological and documentary records of both Cyprus and Ugarit (and the wider Levant where feasible), this study engages several concepts — maritime space and modes of interaction, merchants and mercantilism, agents and actors — in the attempt to gain new insights into the long-term relations between two of the best known, well-connected lands in the Late Bronze Age eastern Mediterranean.

CHAPTER 2

BACKGROUND

As director of the French archaeological mission to Ugarit over many years, Marguerite Yon took a special interest in material and documentary links between Ugarit and Cyprus (so too did her predecessor Claude Schaeffer, of course, but that is another story, presented further below). In a series of publications, she discussed several Cypriot Base-ring *rhyta* found at Ugarit (Yon 1980); Ugarit's maritime trading contacts, including Cyprus, the Levant and Egypt (Yon 1994); material (bronze tripod, pottery) and documentary evidence of relations toward the end of the LBA (Yon 1999a); and the foreign relations of Ugarit with Cyprus (and Crete, the Levant, Egypt) as seen in pottery ('Mycenaean' wares produced on Cyprus as well as Cypriot White Painted V-VI, Base-ring, White Slip and White Shaved wares) and in some written documents related to commercial exchanges or to *Alašiya* (Yon 2003). A more detailed work (Yon 2007) presented once again several of the Akkadian texts from *Alašiya*, some objects inscribed with Cypro-Minoan (as well as a bowl from Hala Sultan Tekke inscribed in Ugaritic cuneiform), and an array of material evidence — e.g., bronze tripods and figurines, a range of pottery styles, ivories, mortuary architecture — associated with daily and cultural practices, architectural features, iconography and maritime cargoes.

Her most recent study of the topic covered much of the same ground, i.e., written and archaeological evidence that attests to relations between the northern Levant and Cyprus at the end of the LBA (Yon 2013). She adds more detail on the Cypro-Minoan documents and on Akkadian texts concerning *Alašiya* — based on four texts published earlier (Nougayrol et al. 1968: 79–89) and on eight new texts recovered during the 1994 excavations in the House of Urtenu at Ras Shamra. Yon (2013: 213–215) also considered similarities in 'cultic' architecture and the use of ashlar masonry seen at Ugarit and at several sites on Cyprus (Enkomi, Kition, Kalavasos, Alassa, Palaepaphos—see Figures 6a, 6b, below, for all sites mentioned in the text). Regarding Cypriot imports, she treated much of the same material discussed in her previous studies: pottery (local wares, 'Mycenaean' wares produced on Cyprus), ivory and metals (and an aside on copper ingots), but here added two small faience stirrup jars, one from Ugarit and one from Kition *Bamboula* (Yon 2013: 216–217, fig. 4a-b).

Virtually all the material and documentary evidence Yon presented in these several publications is discussed elsewhere in this study, according to the type of material or context. It is worthwhile noting, however, that Yon concluded her most recent study by observing that the amount of Cypriot material goods — metals, wood, pottery, luxury items — carried by Cypriot merchants to Ugarit seems to be more prominent and abundant than that of northern Levantine goods carried to Cyprus; in her view, this disparity results more from chance than from the nature of the actual maritime cargoes involved. All these finished goods, raw materials, luxury items and more found at multiple sites circulated "… dans une vaste aire d'expansion commerciale et culturelle assez homogène" (Yon 2013: 218–219).

Yon's views run rather counter to what I argue in this study: there may indeed be some cultural homogeneity between Cyprus and northern Levantine coastal sites but in economic terms, Ugarit was a long-established, key commercial hub where all sorts of raw materials and finished goods were available. Cyprus, by contrast, was a relative newcomer to the eastern Mediterranean commercial sphere; although it clearly provided finished goods (pottery, metal items) to Ugarit, its main and most desirable resource was copper, the essential raw material of the Bronze Age. Consequently, over the course of the LBA, the power dynamic between these two polities changed dramatically.

As one outcome of his excavations at the site of Maroni *Vournes* on Cyprus, Cadogan (1998) argued for what he saw as 'revolutionary' changes on 13th century BC Cyprus. Discounting any specific influences from the Aegean realm, he considered the Canaanite or Syrian impetus to changes in architecture, writing, weight systems, commerce and agriculture, politics and religion. The grid system of streets that he sees at Enkomi (and, less obviously at Kition, Kalavasos *Ayios Dhimitrios* and Sinda) has its clearest parallel at Ras ibn Hani, one of Ugarit's ports (Cadogan 1998: 7). Regarding several monumental, often ashlar-enhanced buildings on Cyprus (e.g., the Ashlar Building and West Building at *Vournes*, Building X at *Ayios Dhimitrios*), he pointed to several possible Levantine parallels and suggested they might be regarded as exemplars of what Wright (1992: 266) once termed the 'Old Mediterranean' type of temple (Cadogan 1998: 7–11). On ashlar masonry as a construction technique, he felt confident that "… the idea is most likely to have come from Syria, where places like Ras Shamra produce close parallels" (Cadogan 1998: 11, citing Hult 1983). Regarding writing practices, he noted that the form, shape and apparent content of Cypro-Minoan inscriptions, as well as their presence at Ugarit, corroborate the notion of close links between these two lands. So too does the appearance of animal-shaped weights that appear in Late Cypriot (LC) IIC contexts, which either had connections to or derived from the Levant.

Cadogan (1998: 11-12) also envisioned some similarities in the technology and storage facilities associated with olive oil production at Ugarit and at several Cypriot sites (Maroni *Vournes*, Kalavasos, Alassa, Myrtou *Pigadhes*). Regarding commercial exchanges, he suggested that some metal goods (including copper oxhide ingots) and various decorative arts (faience, ivory, jewellery, seal stones), as well as Cypriot pottery (especially Base-ring wares), were involved in an eastern Mediterranean commercial and cultural *koiné*. From this system, he felt that Cyprus derived many new ideas, especially regarding writing, ashlar masonry, 'temple' plans and perhaps the grid system of streets. He also observed that the closest material links — possibly reflecting a 'special relationship' — were those shared between Ugarit and Enkomi (Cadogan 1998: 13). Unlike Yon's more considered views, some of Cadogan's suggestions seem difficult to sustain. In any case, all the data presented and discussed by both Yon and Cadogan are taken up elsewhere in this study.

By the LBA, maritime connectivity was well established in the eastern Mediterranean, and ranged from well organised, long-distance trading expeditions to smaller-scale, coastal oriented ventures between a succession of ports and capes (cabotage) (Knapp 2018: 103–165; Leidwanger and Knappett 2018). Moreover, an array of material and documentary evidence from earlier and contemporary periods of the Bronze Age (e.g., Monroe 2011; Murray 2023a), along with a suite of analytical data (e.g., Mountjoy and Mommsen 2015; Knapp and Demesticha 2017; Day et al. 2020), indicate that seaborne trade within the eastern Mediterranean was complex, multi-dimensional and always changing: it involved local as well as state control, entrepreneurial ventures and polity-level gift exchange (Sherratt and Sherratt 1991; Knapp and Cherry 1994: 126–151; Panagiotopoulos 2012). The likelihood that even traders involved in localised, coastal expeditions established gift exchange and other socioeconomic ties seems evident from both ethnographic analogies (e.g., Junker 1999 on the vast network of traders operating in the Philippine archipelago during the first millennium AD) and from related cases in the LBA eastern Mediterranean (Manning and De Mita 1997: 113–115; Knapp and Meyer 2023: 327). Arnaud (2005: 118–121), moreover, and importantly, observed that it is not only essential to distinguish between long-distance trade and cabotage but also to realise that the two were often combined.

Once maritime transport became the common mode for commercial exchange in the eastern Mediterranean (Broodbank 2010), the inhabitants of coastal Syria presumably would have been in regular contact with those living on the island of Cyprus, less than 100 km distant. Such contacts were particularly strong during the LBA, a time when Cyprus became a well-connected node for maritime commerce between the Levant and areas farther west (coastal western Anatolia, the Aegean, Greece, central Mediterranean) (Knapp 2022; Knapp et al. 2022). Anyone who has ever considered the webs of transport, exchange and communication that linked the diverse regions of the eastern Mediterranean during the LBA has emphasized the maritime route between northern Syria — especially Ugarit — and Cyprus (e.g., Hankey 1967; Wachsmann 2000: 811–815, fig. 7; Hirschfeld 2004; 2009; Sauvage 2012: 273–274, and fig. 83; Steel 2013: 30–31; Safadi 2016: 354, and fig. 5). Yon (1999a 113–114) even suggested that the Uluburun shipwreck might have set sail from Ma'ḥadu, Ugarit's main port in the bay at Minet el-Beidha, which served as a centre of Mediterranean commerce and a transit point between maritime traffic and the Levantine interior.

The 13th century BC in particular was a prosperous time for the lands of the eastern Mediterranean, apparent in the rich and diverse material record seen at Ugarit and at many coastal sites on Cyprus. For Bronze Age merchants, Cyprus provided a major source of copper whilst its ports served as ideal places to keep abreast of fluctuations in demand and supply. The market potential of Cypriot ports like Enkomi, Hala Sultan Tekke, Kition and Maroni grew as new connections emerged, giving merchants access to a variety of people and a range of products — domestic and foreign — that helped to ensure the success of their journeys (Knapp and Meyer 2023). Cypriot ships travelled to Ugarit and the wider Levant with cargoes of copper, grain, oil and perhaps wine (Knapp 1983: 42–43).

Enkomi, the Cypriot port nearest to Ugarit, has extensive evidence for urban metallurgy (e.g., Pickles and Peltenburg 1998; Kassianidou 2012), even though it is situated farther from the island's copper ore sources than any other major LBA urban coastal centre. In turn, Ugarit's strategic location enabled it to function as a major market and transhipment centre, one that supplied both copper and tin to other regional centres (Kassianidou 2003: 116; Bell 2012; Dardaillon 2012). Enkomi and other Cypriot ports in the east and southeast of the island (Hala Sultan Tekke, Kition) were instrumental in providing copper to the Levant, but in order to produce bronze goods, the island had to import tin — whatever its origin —from the mainland, most likely from Ugarit.

With this background in mind, in what follows I present more detailed evidence of fieldwork, research and publications related to both Ugarit and Cyprus.

UGARIT

> *Ugarit, an archaeological marvel thanks to the exceptional duration and extent of modern excavations …* [which] *over the last eight decades have revealed about a sixth of the later 2nd millennium BC town …. Ugarit boasted a royal palace, grand mansions, residential quarters with kin groups of rich and poor families living side-by-side, wealthy tombs beneath houses, and tower temples …. The thousands of unearthed tablets cover economic, diplomatic, legal, ritual, literary and mythological matters, an accumulation steeped in local and more distant literary traditions, written in four scripts and eight languages ….* (Broodbank 2013: 391–393).

In a recent network analysis of the so-called collapse at the end of the LBA in the eastern Mediterranean, Linkov et al. (2024) present arguments using data and information from ten politico-economic nodes to determine which scenarios best reflect the then-current historical conditions. Nine of these nodes represent the most important regions of the Late Bronze Age (Cyprus, Canaan, Crete, mainland Greece, Hittite Anatolia, western Anatolia, Egypt, Assyria, Babylonia) whilst the tenth is Ugarit, which they describe as "an international city with substantial archaeological and textual evidence" (Linkov et al. 2024: 3). Their model predicted a complete network failure only if both Ugarit and the Hittite state collapsed simultaneously, a situation that seems plausible based on both documentary and material evidence. Although somewhat anecdotal, this study reflects well the views of contemporary scholarship on the key position and role of Ugarit in the mercantile world of the LBA eastern Mediterranean.

The site of Ugarit, or Ras Shamra (Cape Fennel), is situated some 12 km north of Latakia in present-day northern Syria. A large portion of the site, particularly its LBA levels, has been extensively excavated over the past 75 years (see Broodbank's glowing description above, and further below). These excavations have brought to light a clear town plan from the end of the LBA, with residential quarters arranged into blocks, two

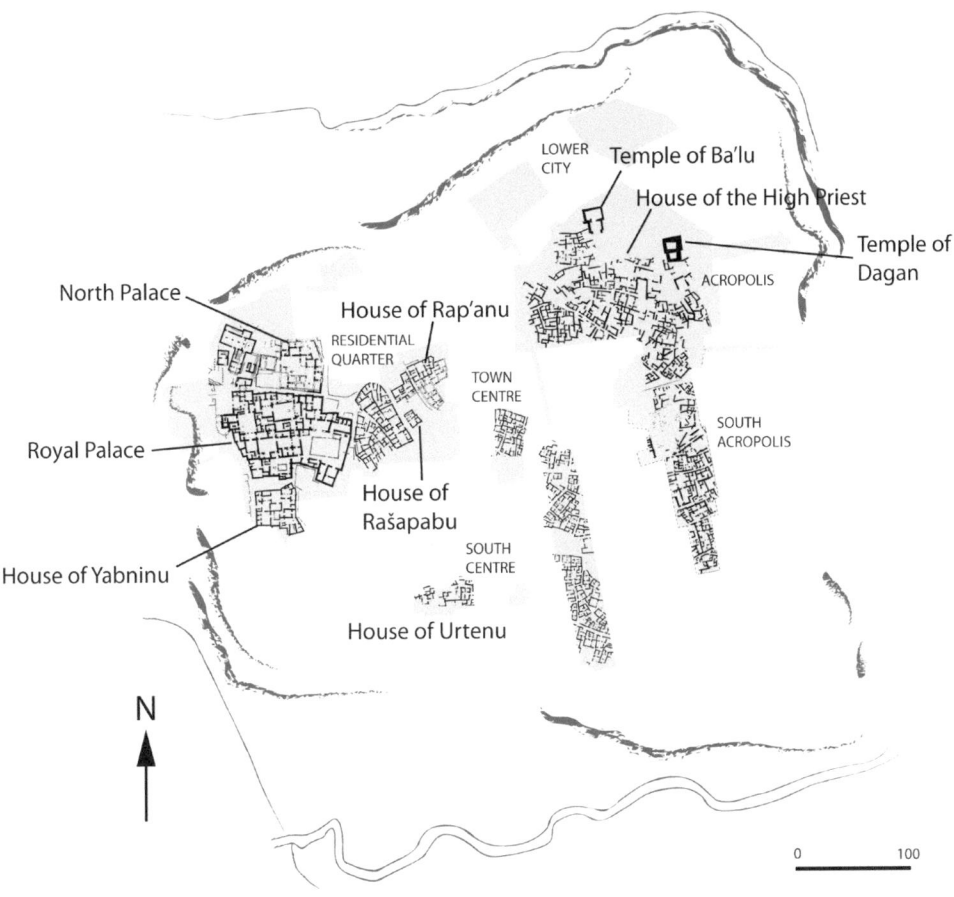

Figure 1. *Plan of town at Ugarit (Boyes 2021: fig. 0.1).*

major temples on the acropolis and an extensive palace sector to the northwest, accessed by one of the city gates (Figure 1) (Boyes 2021: fig. 0.1; see also Broodbank 2013: 392, fig. 837). Several palatial and private archives contain texts (often administrative in nature) — written in Akkadian and the local Ugaritic cuneiform and dated to the 14th and 13th centuries BC — that provide copious information on Ugarit's internal and international relations (Hawley et al. 2015; Pardee 2023; Roche-Hawley 2023).

Yon (2006: 9, 11 fig. 6) maintained that the kingdom of Ugarit extended from the Mediterranean Sea eastward to the Jebel al-Ansariyah mountain range, and from Ras el-Bassit in the north to the border of the *Siyannu* kingdom in the south, an area of approximately 2000 km^2 (Figure 2) (Boyes 2021: fig. 0.2). The site of Ras el-Bassit (ancient *Sinaru*?) lies some 30 km north of Ras Shamra and is regarded by some as the most northerly port of the territory of Ugarit (Pardee 2023: 63 n.70, 96); it is notable for its numerous Cypriot pottery imports (Courbin 1986: 185; Sauvage 2012: 41–42, 298 map 3). The location of *Siyannu* is preserved in the name of the nearby river, Nahr es-Sinn; recently published Akkadian texts from the House of Urtenu portray relations between Ugarit and *Siyannu* (Pardee 2023: 80; Roche-Hawley 2023: 44).

Figure 2. *Map of kingdom of Ugarit (Boyes 2021: fig. 0.2).*

Figure 3. *Minet el-Beidha and Ugarit (Google maps).*

Figure 4. *Minet el-Beidha-80 Canaanite jars (Schaeffer 1939: pl. IX).*

The sandy cove at Minet el-Beidha (White Harbour, ancient *Maʾḫadu*), likely Ugarit's main port, lies about 1 km distant from the tell at Ras Shamra and has been excavated to some extent (Saade 1995; Matoïan 2017; Sauvage and Lorre 2023) (Figure 3). Sauvage (2012: 41–44) offers a more expansive discussion of Ugarit's ports, and elsewhere suggests that the term *maʾḫad* meant 'a place where we can take or find something' (Sauvage 2006: 620). Her view is likely based on Astour (1970: 118–119), who derives the term from Akkadian *māḫāzu*, 'a place of taking, a market city'. Beyond the streets, excavations in several houses and tombs uncovered at Minet el-Beidha produced a range of imports, mainly of Cypriot origin (e.g., White Slip II, White Shaved and Base-ring wares) (for site plan, see several figures in Marchegay 2001; Sauvage and Lorre 2023: 34–36, figs. 4-6). Of striking interest was a batch of some 80 Canaanite jars — the Maritime Transport Container par excellence — found stacked up in a storeroom at Minet el-Beidha, perhaps destined for export (Schaeffer 1939: 3, 30–32, pl. III.3; Sauvage 2006: 618–619, figs. 3-5; 2015: 73; Knapp and Demesticha 2017: 46–66) (Figure 4). Sauvage and Lorre (2023) have recently published a suite of material, mainly from Schaeffer's 1929-1935 excavations at the site, in particular the findspots and interpretation of certain collections held in the Musée d'Archéologie Nationale in Saint-Germain-en-Laye (discussed in detail below).

Excavations at another nearby port about 10 km south, Ras Ibn Hani (variously thought to be ancient *Biʾruti, Appu* or *Raʾšu*— Arnaud 1984; Bounni 2000;

Figure 5. *Copper oxhide ingot. The Metropolitan Museum of Art, Rogers Fund, 1911 (11.140.7). Image courtesy of The Metropolitan Museum of Art.*

Yon 2006: 12; Sauvage 2012: 41; Goiran et al. 2015: 51), revealed an additional, likely royal palace ('South Palace'), prominent houses and tombs (Lagarce and Lagarce 1995; Bounni et al. 1998). The site likely served as a harbour over many millennia, and its Bronze Age levels revealed significant building activity (Goiran et al. 2015: 58–59, fig. 10). Dated to the 13th century BC, a second palatial structure ('North Palace') has been identified; it contained all the textual evidence from the site — some 130 documents, mainly in Ugaritic cuneiform (Boyes 2021: 139–141, figs. 6.15–6.16). Ras ibn Hani also produced various metallurgical installations, as well as pot bellows, crucibles and tuyeres, and the only known example of an oxhide ingot mould — a hollowed-out, calcareous sandstone slab (Lagarce et al. 1983: 277–279, fig. 15; Lagarce and Lagarce 1997; Bounni et al. 1998: 43–48).

Oxhide ingots, of course, are widely regarded as one of the signature material features of LBA Cyprus (Muhly et al. 1988; Gale 1991; Kassianidou 2009; 2023; Graziadio 2014) (Figure 5). Lead isotope analyses suggests that the few drops of copper recovered from the ingot mould were consistent with production from Cypriot ores (Bounni et al. 1998: 44; Dardaillon 2012: 172).

In considering relations between Ugarit and Cyprus, some of the most relevant documentary evidence comes from the so-called merchants' houses (see Figure 1, above). In particular, the merchants Yabninu, Urtenu, Rap'ānu and Rašap-Abu played multiple roles within the polity of Ugarit and operated variously under palatial contract or on a private basis. Along with their families, they were involved in multiple aspects of production and exchange (Monroe 2009: 240, 283; del Olmo Lete 2018) (see further below, in Chapter 7, *The Merchants of Ugarit and Cyprus*).

The House of Urtenu contained the most recently excavated major archive at Ugarit, with some 545 tablets — mainly in Akkadian — that treat international royal correspondence as well as administrative and commercial matters (Bordreuil et al. 2012; del Olmo Lete 2018: 61–62; Pardee 2023: 90, and *passim*; Roche-Hawley 2023). Urtenu's House also contained two Cypro-Minoan 'labels' (Ferrara 2012: 142–144, table 3.4) as well as a range of Monochrome and other Cypriot wares (Sauvage 2012: 179 and n. 1309). Along with Yabninu, Urtenu took part in diverse, private exchange activities involving the import or export of goods from or into Cyprus, the Aegean, Anatolia, Egypt and northern Mesopotamia (McGeough 2015: 91, 93–94). Although merchants like Urtenu likely maintained most of the ships involved in maritime expeditions, the crown also invested in commerce and occasionally taxed merchants. In one transaction, for example, a Cypriot trader sought to purchase ships offered for sale by one of his Ugaritic counterparts, but the king of Ugarit had to sign off on it (Virolleaud 1965: 14–15; Knapp 1983; cf. Pardee 2023: 72). All documentary evidence from Ugarit pertaining to its merchants and related mercantile matters is presented below, in Chapter 6 (*Cyprus and Ugarit: Documentary Evidence*).

CYPRUS

Extending over some 9250km^2, Cyprus is the Mediterranean's third largest island (after Sicily and Sardinia); it lies about 70km south of Turkey, 100km west of Syria and 400km north of Egypt. Rhodes, the closest Aegean island, lies nearly 500km west. The coastline of Cyprus embraces several natural harbours that were home to some of the island's best known Bronze Age sites (e.g., Enkomi, Kition, Hala Sultan Tekke) (Figures 6a, 6b).

The Troodos mountains form the island's main structural and topographic feature (Constantinou 1982: 13–15). Copper ores from the massive sulphide deposits of the Troodos Ophiolite Complex have always been important in socioeconomic and cultural terms, and often have propelled Cyprus's economy over the past 4000 years (see, e.g., Jansen et al. 2018). In addition to the Troodos, which extend over much of the island's south and southwest, Cyprus's main physiographic features are the Kyrenia mountain range in the north, and the central lowland plain, or *Mesaoria* ('between the mountains'). The coastal strip north of the Kyrenia range — never

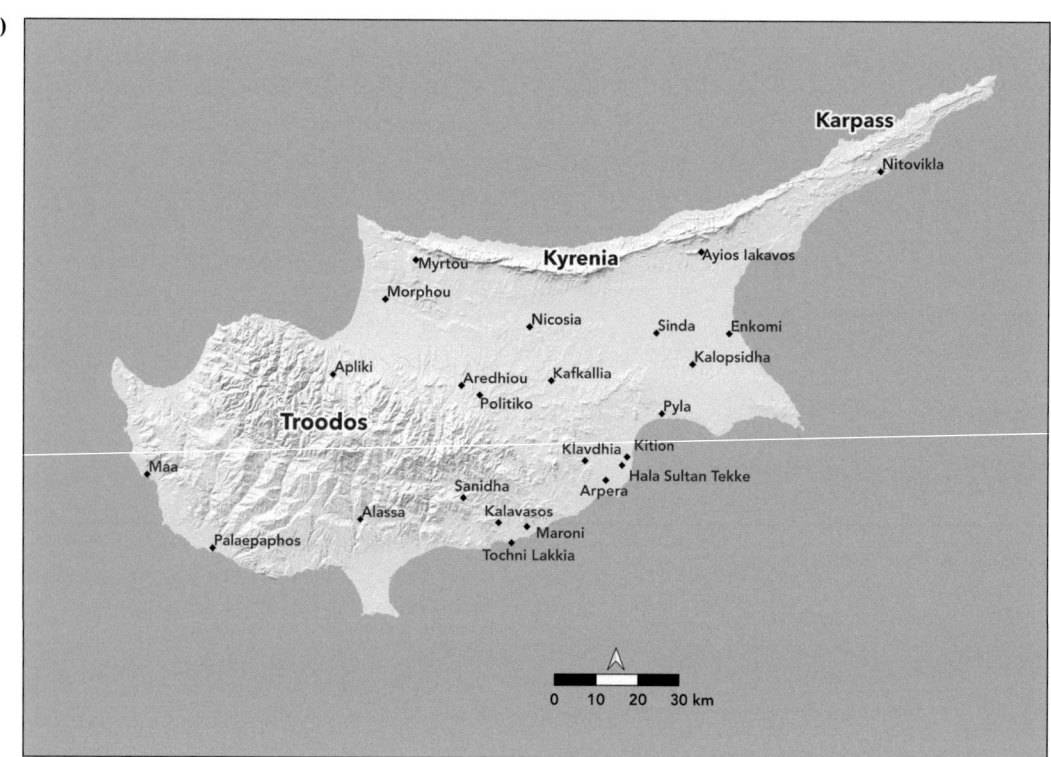

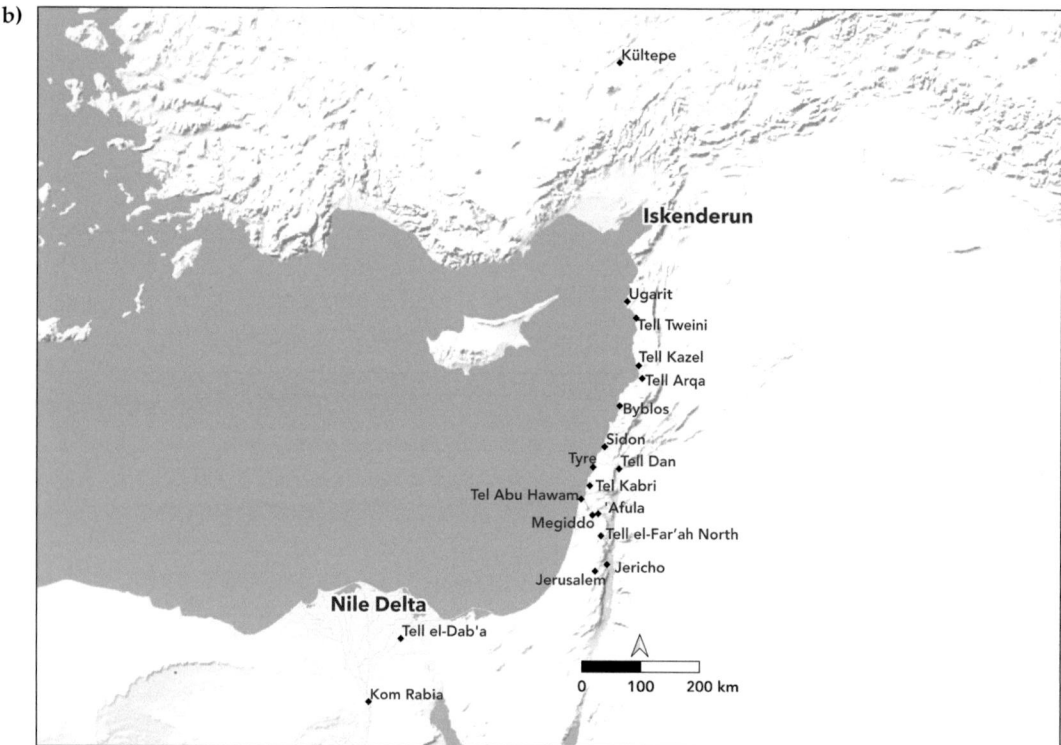

Figure 6. a) *Map of Cyprus, with sites mentioned in text,* **b)** *Map of eastern Mediterranean, with sites and features mentioned in text (both prepared by Nathan Meyer).*

more than 5km wide — is greener and more fertile than the rest of the island. To the east of the Kyrenia range lies the long, finger-like, Karpass peninsula, pointing toward the Bay of Iskenderun (see Figure 6a).

Already during the Middle Cypriot (MC) period (ca. 2000/1900-1650 BC), several material features and related social developments suggest early stages in the rise of a more complex, perhaps even hierarchical polity on the island (Webb and Knapp 2021). From at least the 19th century BC onward, Cyprus's copper ores were exploited for local consumption and at least occasional overseas trade (Knapp 2012: 14–17; Webb and Frankel 2013: 206–213). At the same time, throughout the MC era and continuing into the LC, the people of Cyprus retained a productive agropastoral base that had long underpinned its economy (Andreou 2016, 2019).

The political economy of the LC period (ca. 1650–1100/1050 BC) was increasingly town-centred and industrial in nature. Driven by externally oriented settlements like Enkomi and Hala Sultan Tekke along the island's eastern and southern coasts, intensified copper production and distribution spurred the economy (Knapp 1996a; Kassianidou 2013). Previous studies have demonstrated that the people and the merchants of LBA Cyprus increasingly were engaged through diverse networks of exchange with surrounding peoples and polities in the contemporary Levant, Egypt, Anatolia and the Aegean (e.g., Pieniazek et al. 2018; Knapp and Meyer 2023; Murray 2023b: 414–419, 423–424).

A growing number of imports — e.g., objects of gold, ivory and faience, most often found in mortuary contexts — demonstrate Cyprus's involvement in the international exchange system(s) of the LBA eastern Mediterranean (e.g., Keswani 2004: 136–139; Knapp 2013: 427–432; Bretschneider et al. 2021; Bürge 2021). With respect to exports, in addition to raw materials such as copper and timber, and perhaps purple dye and textiles (Reese 2018: 535–542; Georgiadou and Georgiou 2019; Sauvage 2024), Cyprus continued to send pottery to multiple sites in the Levant, Egypt, Anatolia and the Aegean (e.g., Snape 2003; Maguire 2009; Charaf 2010-11; Bergoffen 2013, 2018, 2023; Papadimitriou 2013; Kozal *et al.* 2020; Spathmann 2021–22; Clark 2024a, 2024b: 105–107).

The people of Cyprus confronted deep social change during the LBA: the growth of urbanisation and the imposing monumental architecture associated with it; alterations in mortuary practices; the emergence of writing in the form of the Cypro-Minoan script (Ferrara 2012; Knapp 2013: 348–432; Webb 2018). The intensified industrialisation and specialisation evident in both metallurgical and pottery production resulted in further economic and social changes (Kassianidou 2008; Steel 2010; Georgiou 2018a; Meyer and Knapp 2021). Settlement numbers as well as site size and diversity also increased, and the population presumably grew as well.

Several prominent new, externally oriented settlements and ports were established along the island's coasts during the LC 1 period (ca. 1650-1450 BC): e.g., Enkomi and Hala Sultan Tekke *Vyzakia*, Episkopi (Kourion) *Bamboula*, *Palaepaphos*, Morphou *Toumba tou Skourou* (see Figure 6a, above). These sites had no significant earlier history, and many were oriented toward the sea; they are well known in the literature (see Knapp 2013: 49–359, with further refs). Other sites that arose in the interior during the LC period were oriented around resource extraction and agricultural production — e.g., Apliki *Karamallos*, Sanidha *Moutti tou Ayiou Serkou*, Aredhiou *Vouppes*, Politiko *Phorades* (Todd 2004: 161–171; Knapp and Kassianidou 2008; Steel 2016; Kassianidou 2018, 2022). The small anchorage revealed by recent, limited excavations at Tochni *Lakkia* (Andreou *et al.* 2019) served in part to distribute agropastoral products around the island, in part as a maritime link that provided goods to larger ports (e.g., nearby Maroni) involved in external, maritime trade.

From the onset of the LBA, ca. 1650 BC, the site of Enkomi functioned as an *emporion*. Excavations at the site have uncovered a wide range of imported goods and specialised products, including Canaanite Jars and Egyptian pottery, ivory and metal products, cylinder seals, jewellery and much more (see, for example, Courtois et al. 1986; Keswani 1989; Crewe 2012: 232–234). To judge from all its material and mortuary remains, archaeometallurgical installations and Cypro-Minoan texts, Enkomi clearly served as one of Cyprus's primary ports of trade and functioned as a crucial nexus in eastern Mediterranean exchange systems. With favourable conditions, Enkomi was likely about one day's sail (some 100 kms) from Ugarit and the northern Levantine coast (Bar-Yosef Mayer et al. 2015: 428); extrapolating from the simulation by Gal et al. (2023), which indicates that the run from Sidon in Lebanon to Kition would have taken roughly 2.5 days on average, the slighter distance from Ugarit may well have taken less time.

Enkomi and Ugarit also share several material features in common: ashlar masonry, urban mortuary practices, stone anchors, use of the Cypro-Minoan script, pottery and artistic expression more generally. Bell (2012: 186) even suggested that once Ugarit had been destroyed (ca. 1200 BC), some of Ugarit's merchants may have translocated to Enkomi. Be that as it may, I turn now to consider the most prominent of these material elements.

CHAPTER 3

UGARIT AND CYPRUS: COMMON MATERIAL FEATURES

ASHLAR MASONRY

The earliest use of this technique on Cyprus is attested at the Nitovikla Fortress during LC IB, ca. 1500 BC (Hult 1992), where ashlar blocks were used to enhance the entrance to the gateway. Beginning some 100 years later, ashlar masonry was employed in the erection of the LC IIA-B built tombs at Enkomi (Keswani 2004: 115; see further below, in *Urban Mortuary Practices*). Excavations at several LC sites — Kition, Maroni *Vournes*, Kalavasos *Ayios Dhimitrios*, Alassa *Paleotaverna* — show that ashlar masonry became more common on Cyprus during the 13th century BC but was not associated chronologically with any notable changes in the overall pottery repertoire (see, e.g., Hult 1983; Cadogan 1984: 8–10; Wright 1992: 228; Lagarce 1993: 100) (Figure 7). Both of Enkomi's major excavators — C.F.A. Schaeffer and P. Dikaios — linked ashlar masonry with the Mycenaeans (Papasavvas 2023: 65).

Hult's (1983: 88–90) essential study on the use of ashlar construction on Cyprus linked it mainly to Syria (with possible Minoan influences). Wright (1992: 411, 520–521) guardedly agreed but felt that the ashlar style of LBA Cyprus was developed locally using masonry devices common to a broad stylistic *koiné*. Hitchcock (2008) also noted the unique aspects of Cypriot ashlar but argued particularly for Minoan influences. Philokyprou (2011) examined the (three) different types of stone and the techniques used in ashlar masonry on LBA Cyprus; he suggested that some features (e.g., drafted margins, orthostats) may also be seen in the ashlar masonry of Minoan Crete and some sites of the Levantine coast, notably at Ugarit. In the most recent survey of the evidence, Fisher (2020: 315) argues that Cypriot elites drew upon both local traditions and architectural elements common throughout the eastern Mediterranean (i.e., ashlar masonry) in creating monumental buildings and adapting them to local modes of social organisation and interaction. It seems evident that there were multiple, globalised

Figure 7. *Ashlar masonry, Building II, Alassa* Paleotaverna *(photo by Bernard Knapp)*.

aspects of ashlar construction in use on Cyprus (Fisher 2020: 315), amongst which Syrian influences were the most prominent.

Early work by Schaeffer (1932, 1935) regarded the large ashlar tombs found at both Ugarit and Minet el-Beidha as Mycenaean in origin; he also suggested the possible colonisation of Ugarit by Aegean or Cypriot merchants (Schaeffer 1933: 115–116). Eventually Schaeffer (1939: 68, 77–97) became more cautious, stressing parallels with the architecture of Minoan Crete. Callot, who became the official architect of the French excavations at Ras Shamra in 1979, produced more critical studies on Ugarit's LBA architecture and building techniques (Callot 1983, 1994). In two studies considering Ugarit's foreign relations, notably with Cyprus, Yon (1999b: 132–133; 2003: 43) did not exclude the possibility of a Cretan origin for the use of ashlar masonry in the eastern Mediterranean but stressed certain similarities with both Mycenaean and Cypriot architectural features. In turn,

Margueron (2008) emphasized the diverse Egyptian, Hittite and Minoan aspects of successive building stages evident in the Royal Palace at Ugarit.

Bessac and Matoïan's (2020) recent, highly detailed and technical study on the use of cut-stone masonry at LBA Ugarit especially, but also in the harbours at Minet el-Beidha and Ras ibn Hani, focuses on specific features such as corbelled vaulting, dovetail clamps, bosses and recessed bands. They see no indicators that the masons of Ugarit adopted a specific foreign technique; instead, they regard Ugarit as a 'testing laboratory' for the adoption and use of ashlar masonry in local buildings (the 'royal palace' and other royal residences, merchant houses), columns and tombs. Specifically, they see a technological evolution harkening back to the Early Bronze Age and involving cultural exchanges with Egypt, Cyprus and Minoan Crete (Bessac and Matoïan 2020: 302).

All these studies tend to echo the situation on Cyprus as Fisher (2020; 2023: 251–259) envisioned it, i.e., the globalised features of ashlar masonry used throughout the eastern Mediterranean during the LBA. Nonetheless, we should also bear in mind the extent to which the architectural traditions of Ugarit, particularly those of its rulers and wealthy merchants, may have influenced their Cypriot counterparts.

URBAN MORTUARY PRACTICES

This section draws extensively upon Keswani's (2012) detailed study of Middle-Late Bronze Age urban mortuary practices at Ugarit and Enkomi. Five ashlar-built, rectangular tombs were concentrated in Enkomi *quartiers* Q3E and Q4E; three of them (British Tomb 1/French Tomb 1409, British Tomb 66/French Tomb 1322, French Tomb 1394) were situated quite close to one another in Q4E.104 (Courtois et al. 1986: 3 fig 1, 25 fig. 4; Keswani 2012: 195). These tombs seem to be aligned with, and situated within the walls of well-built household complexes, beneath a single room of the buildings above (Crewe 2009: 28). This layout may be compared with that of similar tombs at Ugarit, where the main chamber often lay beneath a large room in the overlying building, but typically was accessed through a dromos in an adjacent, smaller room (Salles 1987: 159–160). Not every house in Ugarit had a tomb beneath it; according to Marchegay (2000: 208) the proportion of tombs to houses was roughly 1:2/3, depending on housing density in different areas.

That there are similarities between the ashlar-built tombs of Enkomi and those of Ugarit has long been recognised (e.g., Westholm 1939: 57–58; Keswani 2012: 196; Bessac and Matoïan 2020: 302; Fisher 2020: 315). Keswani (2012: 197) felt that although the Enkomi tombs resemble those of Ugarit, they may represent an intermediate point on the continuum of architectural development in ashlar masonry seen at Ugarit. Nonetheless, the Enkomi tombs lack the type of refined corbelling seen in the 'Mycenaean' tombs found at Ugarit and Minet el-Beidha (e.g., Enkomi British Tomb 66/French Tomb 1322—Murray et al. 1900: 5, fig. 5; Minet el-Beidha Tomb III—Bessac and Matoïan 2020: 274, fig. 10.11; see also Margueron 1977: 176, fig. 13); they also lack some other elaborate architectural features seen at Ugarit, such as arched-top doorways, windows and annexes (Bessac and Matoïan 2020).

Other built tombs, particularly those of *tholos* type, found at LBA Enkomi also have parallels at Ugarit and other Middle-Late Bronze Levantine sites. Taking the evidence from Ugarit first, Keswani (2012: 185) reported that all LBA burials recorded at the site came from built tombs, 205 in number according to Marchegay (2008); an additional eight tombs were found at Minet el-Beidha, where the use of pit or shaft tombs also continued in use. Such skeletal remains as are preserved in these built tombs — some used for several generations — include the burials of men, women and children, numbering from a few to as many as 66 individuals (Marchegay 2008: 110; Keswani 2012: 185, nn. 25-26). Differences in the construction of the overlying houses and tombs, and in the types of grave goods recovered, suggest that Ugarit's built tombs were used by kin groups of both royal and non-royal heritage, reflecting notable but also variable wealth and social prestige (see also Salles 1995: 175; Marchegay 2000: 209). Most tombs at Ugarit seem to have been planned and constructed at the same time that the overlying houses were built (Salles 1987: 160; Callot 1994: 175, 373–377, figs. 278-287); thus, they might be regarded as 'private' in nature, whilst those at Enkomi might be seen as more 'public'.

Beginning in the LC I period (ca. 1650 BC) at Enkomi, tombs were built in open spaces surrounding houses and other architectural complexes. As the settlement at Enkomi expanded, however, some of the earlier tombs were built over by later constructions, even if many could have remained accessible from streets, courtyards and possibly from rooms inside the houses (Keswani 2012: 188, citing Dikaios 1969-1971, pls. 243-248, 266-272; Courtois 1981: 10, fig. 1; Courtois et al. 1986: 25, fig. 4). Tombs of LC I-II date at Enkomi reveal a variety of chamber forms: assymetrical, circular or rounded, 'bilobate' (divided into two or more parts) and square to rectangular (Keswani 2012: 189–190, figs. 6-7). The rectangular tomb form, in particular French Tomb 2 at Enkomi with its ashlar lintels and rock-cut offering pit, may represent an imitation of ashlar tomb forms and furniture seen at contemporary Ugarit (Keswani 2012: 190, n. 69, fig. 8).

During the LC I-II periods (from ca. 1650 to 1250 BC), four or five *tholos*-type tombs with beehive-shaped superstructures were built at Enkomi; they were situated in close proximity to contemporary houses. Keswani (2012: 192–194) noted that these tombs were quite variable in form and in their methods of construction, perhaps drawing inspiration from multiple Levantine examples such as Megiddo Tombs 1 and 2 (beehive-shaped superstructures like that of Enkomi Tomb 21), Tel Dan and Tell Tweini (corbeled tombs with curvilinear to elliptical plans). Tomb A-00170 at Tell Tweini, some 40 km south of Ugarit, held at least 58 individuals, with burial goods including several Cypriot White Painted V jugs and juglets (Hameeuw and Jans 2009: 75–76, fig.1); in Keswani's view, this tomb at Tell Tweini seems to present the closest Levantine parallel for Enkomi Tomb 21.

Like their LBA successors, several stone-built tombs of the late Middle Bronze Age at Ugarit were constructed beneath and more-or-less aligned with the floors of overlying houses. MC or early LC I Cypriot White Painted vessels were recovered in several of these tombs (along with notable amounts of other LC I-II pottery types and a Cypriot hook-tang weapon). Having discussed their layout and other features, Keswani suggested that these early built tombs at Ugarit might have served as 'rough inspiration' for the Enkomi *tholos* tombs, especially Swedish Tomb 21.

In her view: "They were certainly the direct precursors of the ashlar tombs at Ras Shamra, which, in turn, appear to have been the models for the ashlar tombs at Enkomi" (Keswani 2012: 194).

Despite the acknowledged similarities in the urban mortuary practices of Ugarit and Enkomi, it is difficult to determine the social situation(s) that lay behind such commonalities. Were Enkomi's ashlar and tholos tombs the burial vaults of expatriate Syrians as Schaeffer once claimed (Courtois 1969: 97)? Or do they represent the building traditions of Cypriot elites emulating those of their Ugaritic counterparts (Keswani 1989: 55)? As Keswani 2012: 198) noted quite perceptively, perhaps these tombs — both at Ugarit and Enkomi — were constructed "… by kin groups who identified themselves with an international merchant class whose members were linked by marriage as well as trading alliances." I return to consider this point further below.

COMPOSITE ANCHORS

Honor Frost carried out a series of pioneering studies on stone anchors and their significance in the wider Mediterranean, especially on Cyprus (Frost 1963, 1970, 1972, 1985, 1991). Having examined closely the anchors from Ugarit and Kition on Cyprus, she suggested that some of the largest ships that sailed the LBA eastern Mediterranean must have been of Levantine and Cypriot origin (Frost 1985; 1991: 370–371). Although Wachsmann (1998: 211–212) cautioned that it was problematic to identify the port of origin or ethnic affiliation of wrecked ships, he felt that a ship's anchors might offer the most secure evidence. Having conducted stable carbon and oxygen isotope analyses as well as petrography on 17 Middle-Late Bronze Age stone anchors from underwater assemblages along Israel's Carmel coast, Macke et al. (2023) argued for their (mainly) local production, without suggesting any links to individual shipwrecks or port origins. Most scholars, moreover, maintain that it is inappropriate to assign a specific type of anchor to a single region or culture (Toth 2002; Howitt-Marshall 2012: 109; Harpster 2013).

Leaving those critiques to one side for the moment, Frost (1985: 283–284, fig. 1) divided Mediterranean pierced stone anchors into three types: (1) sand anchors (with multiple holes for wooden pieces); (2) weight anchors (with a single hole for the mooring cable); and (3) composite anchors (with three holes, for the mooring cable and wooden arms). Most sailing ships probably held more than one type, to facilitate anchoring on different types of sea floor (e.g., sandy or rocky bottoms). As Miller et al. (2023) have shown in experiments designed to estimate the size of ancient ships (using single-holed examples), heavier anchors are required when anchoring on sand as opposed to anchoring on flat rocks. Some smaller, single-holed anchors might also have functioned as line weights, spaced along a mooring cable, with a larger, composite anchor at the end. One crucial difference between stone weights used at sea and on land is that the former typically have holes or extra piercings for holding wooden arms (Frost 1991: 366).

Although generally following the methodology of Frost's investigations, Votruba (2019) refined the terminology of stone anchors and considered the reasons that lay behind the contemporaneous presence and use of two distinct anchor types in the LBA eastern Mediterranean: (1) the 'pierced stone anchor' (PSA) and (2) what he terms the 'planar stone-frame staked anchor' (PSFSA). Frost (1963: 7–9; 1993: 449–451; 2004: 329) had suggested that the two distinct types would have been used on different types of sea floor, the PSA for rocky cases, the PSFSA primarily for sandy bottoms. Tackling the issue from different perspectives, Votruba argues that Levantine sailors used the PSA from at least the third until the first millennium BC, their dominance ending only when the stock anchor was invented. He also suggested that PSFSA first appeared on Cyprus during the 15th century BC and likely continued to be used by Cypriot (not Levantine) sailors until the end of the Bronze Age (Votruba 2019: 231–232, fig. 9). Thus, in his view, Levantine or Near Eastern sailors had been using the PSA for a millennium or more prior to the (Cypriot) invention of the PSFSA.

Some 73% of the PSF3SA-type stone anchors dated to the second millennium BC were found 'west of the Levant,' and two-thirds of the entire assemblage was found on Cyprus (Votruba 2019: 233). One PSF3SA-type from Israel is inscribed with a Cypro-Minoan sign (Galili and Rosen 2015: fig. 46). Another example of this type of anchor from Ugarit (Frost 1969: table 1, no. 5) also has markings associated with the Cypro-Minoan script (McCaslin 1980: 47; but cf. Frost 1991: 377). Indeed, all six known stone anchors bearing Cypro-Minoan signs are of the PSF3SA-type (listed in Votruba 2019: 234). Based on factors such as form, shape or provenance of the stone used, Votruba (2019: 233) estimated that 75% of the PSF3SA-type anchors datable to the 2nd millennium BC were either found on Cyprus or have been attributed to it. Of particular interest for the present study is that all other examples of this type of anchor derive from either Ugarit or its port Minet el-Beidha.

Finally, during the period of time between the late 15th through early twelfth centuries BC, all known examples of the PSF3SA type were found on Cyprus, either at Hala Sultan Tekke or at Kition, or farther west at Kommos on Crete (two examples—Shaw 1995: 280, fig. 1) and on the LBA Point Iria shipwreck in the Aegean (one example—Vichos 1996: 19, fig. 3a). As a qualifying note, it is necessary to point out that 24 examples of PSA-type have been found on Cyprus, all in land contexts at the site of Kition and thus all dated to the LC II period (Votruba 2019: 234). Perhaps Cypriot sailors made use of both types of stone anchor, i.e., for different types of sea floor as Frost had suggested. Alternatively, Votruba (2019: 234) suggests that LBA Levantine sailors may have had particular incentive to sail to Cyprus, specifically for its copper resources, and that the PSAs found at Kition thus would have been made and dedicated there by Levantine sailors. He thus echoes a recent study by Lamaze (2022: 119–120), who suggests — rather uncritically — that Kition's 'temple precinct' might have been a stopping-off point for Levantine merchant-mariners making their first stop on a journey westward. In the end, however, associating a specific type of anchor to a single region or culture remains problematic and, as Harpster (2013: 617) observed, such an approach tends to ignore the multicultural nature of seafaring activity and "disenfranchises other cultures present on a ship by promoting only one."

As already noted, several of the composite anchors are incised with Cypro-Minoan signs, suggesting a Cypriot origin, and I turn now to consider more closely the Cypro-Minoan script.

CYPRO-MINOAN SCRIPT

The Cypro-Minoan (CM) script was long attested only on Cyprus and at Ugarit, but now is also represented on inscriptions from Tiryns in the Argolid (Vetters 2011; Davis et al. 2014), on the Hishuley Carmel shipwreck off the coast of Israel (Valerio and Davis 2017: 136–137, figs. 6-7) and the Cape Gelidonya shipwreck (Hirschfeld and Bass 2013: 102), and at Ashkelon in the southern Levant (Cassandra Donnelly, pers. comm., April 2024).

Masson (1974) originally classified four different variants of CM. The oldest signs were designated CM 0 (or Archaic CM). The inscriptions found on Cyprus fell mainly into her CM I class; CM II comprised the signs on clay tablets from Enkomi whereas CM III referred to signs found on some of the material from Ugarit. Countering Masson, Palaima (1989; 2005) maintained that the CM signs represent one script denoting one language, and that differences in the occurrence of signs or in the ductus of Masson's three variants only indicated temporal, scribal or material differences. Ferrara (2012: 263, 270–271) also suggested, cautiously, that CM signs — no matter how diverse the script — may represent one language. At Ugarit during the LBA, CM was one of five different scripts used to record eight different languages (Akkermans and Schwartz 2003: 338).

On Cyprus, the CM script turns up in multiple contexts (domestic, mortuary, ceremonial) at both coastal and inland sites. Enkomi has produced by far the largest number of inscribed objects (55% of the approximately 250 known CM inscriptions) and is one of only two sites where CM is found inscribed on tablets (6 fragments), the other being Pyla *Kokkinokremmos* (2 fragmentary examples) (Karageorghis and Kanta 2014: 110–111; Ferrara 2016: 228–229; Bretschneider et al. 2023: 71, and *passim* for other CM marks found at Pyla; see also Hirschfeld 2014: 170–173, fig. AII.5). Inscribed clay cylinders have been found only on Cyprus — at Enkomi and Kalavasos *Ayios Dhimitrios* (5 at the latter site—Masson 1983; Smith 2002: 20–25, fig. 5; Ferrara 2012: 80–81, fig. 2.12). In turn, Ugarit is the only other site where CM-inscribed tablets are found. Ferrara (2012: 132–144) listed three fragmentary and one complete (but damaged) CM tablets, and in addition some other objects inscribed with CM: two 'labels' (or sealings) from the House or Urtenu, a silver bowl and a pithos rim (see also Yon 1999a: 117 fig. 4; Palaima 1989: 158). Here we might add that Valério (2014: 117) mentions a CM inscribed ('plainware?') handle from Ugarit, and caution that Steele (2019: 204) regards the signs on the silver bowl from Urtenu's house "…as a dubious example of Cypro-Minoan writing." Nonetheless, all CM texts found at Ugarit come from private archives in the residences of court officials or administrators closely associated with the kingdom.

In her comprehensive discussion of the clay ball with a CM inscription found at Tiryns, Vetters (2011: 11–12, n. 99) also mentioned two clay balls (*boules*) from Ugarit that seem comparable to Cypriot examples in their dimensions and type, although both are inscribed in alphabetic cuneiform, not CM. Ferrara (2015: 112–113) expanded discussion of these two clay balls and concluded that the signs recorded personal names. In general, Ferrara (2016: 230–231, 242) felt that the CM texts from Cyprus give the impression of being 'haphazardly dispersed', excepting the concentrations of the clay *boules*, primarily at Enkomi but also at Kalavasos *Ayios Dhimitrios*. Nonetheless, she concluded that although Cypriot scribes may be indistinguishable as a professional class, they had attained levels of literacy sophisticated enough to create their own script and to use that script for elite display and self-celebration.

Based on earlier work originating with Olivier Masson and discussed by Egetmeyer (2013), Ferrara (2012: 251–254; 2016: 237) noted that the palaeography of CM inscriptions found at Ugarit seems odd, with up to 12 syllabograms distinct from the known CM sign repertoire (Duhoux 2013). Smith (2003: 284–285), too, noted that the CM inscriptions from Ugarit seem to emulate Ugaritic epigraphic preferences. Be that as it may, of 12 known CM inscriptions from Ugarit, four are tablets — one intact, the others fragmentary (Ferrara 2016: 233–234). Ferrara maintained that two of these tablets — found in the Houses of Rašap-Abu (a harbour-master) and Rap'ānu (an important merchant and scribe) in the residential quarter of the town — were produced and inscribed locally; i.e., they were not sent from Cyprus (see also Ferrara 2012: 136–141). Both Rašap-Abu and Rap'ānu, however, seem to be closely associated with Cyprus: Rap'ānu's residence contained much of the *Alašiya* correspondence in Akkadian (RS 20.168, RS 20.18, possibly RS L.1, RS 20.238—Nougayrol et al. 1968: 79–90; see further below), and two Cypriot seal impressions were recovered from Rašap-Abu's house (van Soldt 1989). Of further relevance is that petrographic analysis of letter RSL 1 from Rap'ānu's house indicates a likely Cypriot provenance (Goren et al. 2003: 238–240).

The other two CM tablets from Ugarit stemmed from the residence of Yabninu, another wealthy merchant who also had close commercial connections with Cyprus (Singer 1999: 677; Ferrara 2012: 134–136). These tablets were written in a style reminiscent of that found on the clay *boules* of Cyprus and recorded CM numerals as well (Ferrara 2015; 2016: 234–235). If Ferrara is correct in suggesting that Ugarit's main concern with Cyprus involved the recording of administrative details concerning exchange matters, then the two tablets found in the House of Yabninu may have been the result of such operations and so may have originated on Cyprus. Although Steele (2019: 202–206) is more cautious overall in her consideration of the context(s) and significance of the CM documents found at Ugarit, she concedes that the frequent occurrence of the term *Alašiya* and the lists of Cypriot personnel mentioned in other documentary evidence from Ugarit indicate close contacts between LBA Cyprus and northern Syria (Steele 2019: 206).

Indeed, close ties between Cyprus and Ugarit are evident not only in the CM inscribed objects found at Ugarit but also in Akkadian and Ugaritic cuneiform documents from the site (Knapp 2008: 319–324, 330–331; see further below, in Chapter 6, *Cyprus and Ugarit: Documentary Evidence*). For example, an unnamed scribe from Ugarit attached to the royal household of *Alašiya* requested that his lord (king of Ugarit) send him some furniture (RS 94.2177+2491) (Lackenbacher and Malbran-Labat 2016: 39). Ferrara (2009: 260) once suggested that the Akkadian cuneiform tablets sent from *Alašiya* to Ugarit may have been composed by scribes specifically trained in the cuneiform tradition of Ugarit (see also Ferrara 2012: 62). As already noted, the presence of CM inscribed tablets in the archives of Rašap-Abu, Rap'ānu and Yabninu also accords well with the notion of intimate cultural and commercial relations between Cyprus and Ugarit at the end of the Bronze Age (Ferrara 2012: 144–145; 2016: 233–234, see also Vincentelli 1976), as do the vast quantities of Cypriot pottery found throughout Syria, particularly at Ugarit.

CHAPTER 4

Cypriot Material in Ugarit

Amongst the wide array of Cypriot material evidence uncovered at Ugarit over nearly 100 years of excavations, seals (and seal impressions), metals and pottery form the focus of discussion in this section. Amongst other common material features, however, Sauvage (2024) recently has pointed out that a range of differently weighted spindle whorls are present both at Enkomi and Ugarit. For example, several 'light' whorls made of bone or ivory were recovered in prestigious contexts at both sites: from Ugarit ('dépôt 43', the royal palace and the *Maison aux Albâtres*); from Minet el-Beidha (tomb III); and from Enkomi (Area I, various tombs) (Sauvage 2024: 32, with further refs.). Another spindle whorl from Ugarit now in the Louvre (AO 14 827), whose decoration was replaced (or crossed out?) by a deeply engraved 'X', finds a loose parallel at Enkomi (ENK 1958) that bears an 'XOX' motif, although the 'O' is a perforation (Sauvage 2024: 42, fig. 13a, b).

In addition, mention should be made of the two or three, finely cut stone 'bathtubs' recovered from LBA levels at Ugarit (Matoïan and Carbillet 2017). These objects were found in rooms — assumed to be toilets — associated with some of Ugarit's more elaborate buildings (*grandes demeures*), namely the *Palais Sud* and a house located just north of the *Maison du Grand-Prêtre* (Matoïan and Carbillet 2017: 215 fig. 4, 227 fig. 19). The authors provide detailed examples of comparanda from both Cyprus and the southern Levant but question their use as markers of origin or ethnicity. Regarding their possible functions — e.g., for bathing, for use in libation or purification rituals, for reinforcing fibres in making wool, or for lanolin extraction in producing perfumes (Mazow 2014), Matoïan and Carbillet take no stance. Concerning relations between Ugarit and Cyprus, they emphasize that these stone objects begin to appear toward the end of the LBA in both places, but again do not indicate if they regard them as imports or the result of local production. Collard (2008), however, has argued strongly for their temporal priority on Cyprus: the earliest examples of these 'bathtubs' on the island can be dated to LC IIA (beginning about 1450 BC), and they continued to be produced throughout the 13th and early 12th centuries BC.

SEALS AND SEAL IMPRESSIONS

Excavations at Ugarit and Minet el-Beidha have produced more cylinder seals regarded as Cypriot in style than all other Levantine sites combined. In a recent study of Cypriot seals found overseas, Smith (2022) devoted one section to 19 cylinder seals found at Ugarit, examining their contexts (merchants' houses) and uses, and considering how they might be related to Cypriot activity at that site. This section draws extensively on Smith's recent study.

Of over 500 stone cylinder seals found at Ugarit and Minet el-Beida, Amiet (1992) regarded 35 as being of Cypriot style, but Smith (2022: 215–220) felt that only 19 of these could reasonably be compared with seal designs and iconography associated with Cyprus. The iconography seen on both Elaborate and Derivative style Cypriot cylinder seals was foreign in derivation but associated with local ideological and political constructs (Webb 1999: 276; 2002: 117–126). Indeed, the very concept of the cylinder seal is not local to Cyprus, and many bear Levantine or Near Eastern design elements (Keswani 1989: 69–70). Amongst the 19 seals discussed by Smith are some Elaborate style seals of hard stone, whilst other, soft stone seals portray scenes of a woman, griffin and tree. The latter group of seals shows several different carving styles like those of some seals found on Cyprus, for example at Episkopi and Enkomi. Smith (2022: 216–218, nn. 86-89, fig. 3b) felt this might indicate not just Ugaritic connections with Cyprus, but also specific links with more than one part of the island.

Six hematite seals, dated ca. 1450-1350 BC, were found in habitational contexts, one in association with a tomb at the House of Rap'ānu who, as already noted, had an archive of some 200 tablets, including a CM tablet and much of Ugarit's known correspondence with Cyprus (van Soldt 2000: 233–234; Boyes 2021: 130–133). Another seal (Amiet 1992: no. 454) showing the upper part of a bearded figure and what may be an added script sign, could be of Levantine or Mesopotamian origin but had been recut with Cypriot Elaborate style figures. These finely cut seals from Ugarit thus may be only partly Cypriot in design (Schaeffer 1983: 48; Smith 2022: 215–216).

Amongst the seal impressions found at Ugarit are two of Elaborate style from the House of Rašap-Abu (Schaeffer 1968: 612–618, nos. RS 17.149, RS 17.36). Both examples had been impressed onto legal tablets written in Akkadian and dealing with the clients and family of Rašap-Abu, a 'harbour-master' of the 13th century BC (van Soldt 2000: 231–232, 243). One of two labels found in the House of Urtenu, which has two CM signs on one side (Yon 1995: 439–441, figs. 7a–b, no. R.S. 94.2328; Ferrara 2012: 142–144), has a seal impression on the opposite side, for which Smith (2022: 219, figs. 4a-b) finds parallels on softer stone examples from Cyprus (e.g., from Kalavasos *Ayios Dhimitrios*).

The ownership and design of seals embedded long biographies that can be informative about the meaning of Cypriot seals found overseas. Whereas these seals and sealings cannot be linked definitively to people or traders from Cyprus, there are obvious associations between their contexts and the Ugaritic merchants — Rap'ānu, Rašap-Abu, Urtenu — closely involved in (social, economic) connections with the island. In Smith's (2022: 220) view, "The Cypriot seals at Ugarit suggest that there was an integral relationship between Cypriots and Ugarit, perhaps more so than anywhere else in the Eastern Mediterranean."

METALS

Multiple streams of evidence indicate that the main source of copper distributed through Ugarit or used in Ugarit's bronze industry originated on Cyprus (Courtois 1976: 24; Sauvage 2012: 152), not least the already-mentioned oxhide ingot mould from Ras Ibn Hani (Lagarce et al. 1983: 277–279, fig. 15). Excavations at Ras ibn Hani also produced various metallurgical installations, as well as pot bellows, crucibles and tuyeres (Bounni et al. 1998). Nonetheless, and although Matoïan and Vita (2020: 21) state that "The wealth of metallic material brought to light from the sites of Ras Shamra and Minet el-Beida, as well as from Ras Ibn Hani, has been highlighted several times" (without references), publications concerning the presence at Ugarit of Cypriot tools, weapons and other metal items are somewhat limited or inaccessible (e.g., two PhD dissertations that treat related topics—Marchegay 1999; Dardaillon 2006).

Matoïan and Vita's (2020) paper itself, however, is quite informative. For example, they note the presence and variety of copper, silver and (predominantly) lead ingots (with reference to the unpublished Dardaillon 2006 thesis). Schaeffer (1931: 7) had cited a 10kg copper ingot from the 1930 excavations at Ugarit; it was subsequently lost but has now been identified with a ring-shaped object in the Louvre, inventory no. AO 13160 (Matoïan and Vita 2020: 34–35, fig. 3). This object might be a weight instead of an ingot, but whatever its function there is nothing to indicate a Cypriot origin (contra Matoïan and Vita 2020: 36 and n.41). That is not the case, however, with what appear to be two fragments of an oxhide-shaped ingot (RS 22.293), found in the northern part of the *tranchée Ville Sud*, which may have been a metal workshop (Matoïan and Vita 2020: 32–33, fig. 2; see also Lagarce and Lagarce 1997: 77, n.12). In a separate study, Dardaillon (2008) mentioned some matte and a copper ingot "found not far from the *bibliothèque* of Ras Shamra" (citing Schaeffer 1936a: 99), as well as copper slag from Minet el-Beidha. Her aim in that study was to compare metallurgical analyses with geological, archaeological and textual data, but the outcome was inconclusive, neither confirming nor discounting a Cypriot origin for these materials.

Matoïan and Vita (2020: 21–22) mention that a large variety of bronze tools, weaponry, jewellery, figurines and vases have been found both in isolation and in groups. For our purposes, of the three references they cite, the most informative is Dardaillon's (2012) study of metal workshops at second millennium BC Ugarit. She lists several tools — 6 spatulae, 3 shovels, 6 tongs, 1 hammer — that are similar to counterparts found in various Cypriot hoards, and she notes some of the Cypriot parallels (Dardaillon 2012: 171, fig. 18.3, 176 nn. 5-6). From the *quartier résidentiel* came tuyères, crucibles and slag, whilst other metallurgical materials were found in the *tranchée Ville Sud* (moulds, a tuyère, the two copper oxhide ingot fragments mentioned above) and the royal palace, and at Minet el-Beidha (Dardaillon 2012: 172, fig. 18.4, 176 n.8; see also Callot 1994: 187; Saade 1995: 217; Chanut 2000: 250). From a *cachette* at Minet el-Beidha came a tanged dagger, some axes and hoes, sickles, tongs and a large shovel with a spiral handle that Courtois (1979: 1286) associated with tools from a metal foundry at Enkomi. Dardaillon (2012: 174–175) also noted some fragmentary metal figurines from the *temple Hourrite*, whose best parallels — in her view — come from Cypriot sites such as Enkomi and Kition.

In a study presenting some of the main finds from monuments on the acropolis at Ugarit, Matoïan (2018: 262–263, fig. 6, 293) discussed several metal items, not least a deposit of 74 bronzes discovered in the *Maison du Grand-Prêtre* during the first season of excavations at Ugarit (1929). Amongst these bronzes was a small (12 cm in height) tripod stand (Louvre AO 11606), almost certainly Cypriot in origin (Courtois 1976: 27; 1979: 1157; Matoïan 2018: 263–264, fig. 7, 293); another, miniature bronze tripod was found in the *Temple aux Rhytons* (RS 80.5102— Yon 1999a: 115, fig. 1). Matoïan (2018: 293, 295 fig. 20) also mentioned and illustrated a bronze tripod support stand (RS 17.93, Damas 3592), found near the *Maison du Grand-Prêtre*. Caubet and Yon (2001: 149–150, fig. 1a) described a silver cup with a short Cypro-Minoan inscription (RS 3.389, Louvre AO 14747); the precise find spot of that silver cup remains uncertain (Schaeffer 1932: 23; Matoïan 2018: 267–269).

In discussing an Ugaritic text (RS 94.2401) that mentions the amounts of copper and tin needed for the manufacture of objects termed *karkubbûma* (Roche-Hawley 2023: 43 transliterates this term *karkābūma*), Bordreuil (2007: 96–98) pointed out that the quantities of copper and tin (11% tin) used to produce them was of the proper ratio to make good quality bronze. He concluded that *karkubbûma* might have functioned either as a metal framework for the burning platform of an altar or as some sort of wheeled frame designed to contain a brazier, i.e., as heaters for large rooms.

Zukerman (2012) discussed these objects at length, suggested that they were produced locally in Ugarit, and argued that they should likely be regarded as bronze wheeled stands, the best known and most widely attested of which derive from Cyprus (see, e.g., Catling 1964: 203–213). More relevant here are Zukerman's (2012: 494, 497) observations that the technological expertise for producing wheeled stands must have resulted from the close economic ties between Cyprus and Ugarit in 13th and 12th centuries BC, and that Ugarit's bronzeworking industry was so sophisticated and well established that it was able to manufacture 40 such costly objects, presumably for the town's elites. Vita (1999: 488) and Monroe (2009: 271–272) also alluded to the vitality of the local metal industry, and noted various Ugaritic documents that mention coppersmiths, metal casters, boilermakers and perhaps jewellers.

This brief overview of metals tools, utensils, weaponry, jewellery and figurines of likely Cypriot origin or design found at Ugarit once again highlights the myriad material, commercial and social links between these two lands throughout the LBA. Moreover, it must be emphasized that this snapshot of likely Cypriot metal goods and objects from Ugarit provides no more than an impression of the items exchanged; the actual numbers must have been significantly greater.

POTTERY

Any attempt to assess the amount and various types of Cypriot material uncovered at Ugarit is hampered by the uneven publication of the first 40 years of excavations at the site; this observation holds especially true for the pottery. C.F.A. Schaeffer served as director of the Mission Archéologique d'Ougarit from 1929-1969, and to his credit provided preliminary reports in the journal *Syria* up to the beginning of the Second World War, and later also in the *Revue d'art oriental et d'archéologie* and in *Comptes rendus de l'Académie des Inscriptions et Belles-Lettres* (see: https://www.mission-ougarit.fr) (Matoïan 2021a: 5–6).

The first volume in the series *Ugaritica—Études relatives aux découvertes de Ras Shamra* appeared in 1939 (Schaeffer 1939). Two further publications presented some of the pottery excavated under Schaeffer's directorship: *Ugaritica* II (Schaeffer 1949), which catalogued finds from 1929-1938, and *Ugaritica* VII (Courtois and Courtois 1978), which dealt with finds made between 1959-1968. Further ceramic material from excavations carried out by M. Yon in 1978-1984 (*Centre de la ville*) and subsequently (*Maison au Sud du Temple aux Rhytons*) were published, respectively, in Yon (1987: 11–127) and in Yon and Arnaud (2001: 83–190).

Bell (2006: 31–37) summarised what she felt were some challenges in engaging data from the early excavations at Ugarit. In her perusal of the literature, for example, she noted that only two out of 38 tombs excavated at Ras Shamra and Minet el-Beidha were undisturbed. She also mentioned problems with the recording of contexts or find spots, the selective and only partial publication of the pottery, and stratigraphic issues (Yon first established a consistent horizontal grid when she assumed the directorship in the late 1970s). Schaeffer seldom treated complete ceramic assemblages but instead concentrated on the more impressive finds. Consequently, early publications on the excavations at Ugarit gave the impression that Mycenaean or Cypriot wares were predominant: this view was only corrected after the 1975-1976 excavations, when Monchambert (1983, 2004) showed that Mycenaean and Cypriot wares combined amounted to no more than 1% of the total amount of pottery in a specific LBA residential context (the amounts from mortuary contexts were notably higher—Yon et al. 2000: 3).

Other, related problems are also evident. For example, in discussing an estimated 1000 Canaanite Jars excavated at Ugarit, Matoïan and Vita (2018: 305 n. 35) stated: "It is difficult to make an exact calculation since the finds made during the excavations under the direction of Claude Schaeffer are far from being itemized completely" (but cf., for example, Al-Maqdissi and Matoïan 2008). They also pointed out, generously, that some of the pottery mentioned in the archives or in publications has yet to be located in museums, not least because "it would seem that the excavator did not preserve all the pottery that was unearthed" (Matoïan and Vita 2018: 313 n. 79). These authors also emphasized the lack of information concerning the *grandes jarres* from the palace *magasins*, noting that most topographic points given on the various loci correspond to many and diverse objects other than the jars themselves (e.g., tablets, weights, bronze weapons, Mycenaean or Cypriot wares, amber and stone beads, an ivory knob, etc.) (Matoïan and Vita 2018: 314 n. 81).

Finally, they indicate another conundrum (Matoïan and Vita 2018: 314):

> *In 2008, we had envisaged that the excavator had not preserved the pottery (following a selective procedure). We are now presented with another hypothesis in view of the finds made in 2009 in the 'Palais Sud' ('Maison de Yabninu'). When study of this building was resumed (as preparation for a detailed publication), work on the ground has shown, in fact, that the large storage jars (or pithoi) of rooms 216 and 219, brought to light in the mid-twentieth century, had been preserved in situ.*

In other words, not only did Schaeffer selectively choose what to publish, he often failed to indicate whether he had even excavated, much less preserved, some of the site's most diagnostic and (to us, at least) most significant materials. This discussion could be prolonged but suffice it to say that even Schaeffer's successors in the French excavations at Ugarit continue to be stymied by the field practices of their predecessor. Schaeffer, of course, also excavated at Enkomi on Cyprus, beginning in 1932 but interrupted by the Second World War; he returned to excavate there in 1946 (Matoïan 2021b: 7) but that is another story, to which I return below (and see now Papasavvas 2023).

So, what can one say about the amount and types of Cypriot pottery found in the excavations at Ugarit, Minet el-Beidha and Ras ibn Hani (see Table 1)?

First of all, in most of the publications that treat Cypriot materials from these sites, the context of some finds is provided, ranging from various structures or tombs to specific findspots (e.g., '*secteurs*', '*Tr. Est* 38-39', '*point top.* 4633', etc.). Whilst a more focused, contextual analysis would surely prove to be more informative, the aim here is to provide an indicative impression — not a quantitative assessment — of the Cypriot pottery found at Ugarit and its main ports; given the state of the published material, it is difficult to attempt more. Even then, however, one is confronted with the problem that some of same materials seem to be cited in different publications with little cross-referencing (but cf. Sauvage and Lorre 2023), thus raising the spectre of overestimating the amount of material.

In *Ugaritica* II (finds from 1929-1938—Schaeffer 1949: 131–301, figs. 50-131), all LBA material from both Ras Shamra and Minet el-Beidha is presented — typically by tomb or other deposits — in a descriptive and chronological manner. Over 80 figures provide mainly drawings (a few photos), some illustrating 30 or more sherds on a single figure. Since the material is presented by its findspot, local wares as well as Cypriot, Mycenaean, Minoan, Anatolian and Levantine pottery are all mixed together and there is no concordance that might offer some impression of the actual amounts of the different wares. The closest we're ever likely to come to comprehending the quantity of Cypriot material — surely hundreds of examples — excavated during those years comes from Schaeffer's own statement (1949: 132, loosely translated, emphasis added):

> *During the Late Bronze, from about 1550 onward, there is an* exceptional *quantity of pottery from the neighbouring island of Cyprus, known for the quality of its ceramic arts and the activities of its workshops.*

	Base-ring	Bucchero	Grey/Black Lustrous Wheelmade	Monochrome	Plain White	Plain White Wheelmade	Red Lustrous	Red-on-Black	Rude/Pastoral Style	White Lustrous	White Painted	White Shaved	White Slip	Wall Brackets
Courtois and Courtois 1978														
230–231 and fig. 9C								1						
256–257 and fig. 20							14							
282–285 and fig. 30: 22													22	
324–331, figs. 43, 45									12					
Yon 1987														
40, 46, 52, 55, figs. 21, 35-36, Maison A	3				1								2	
74, 81, 83, 85, figs. 57, 61 Maison B					1			1					3	
97, fig. 76, Maison E							4							
Yon and Arnaud 2001														
94-96, 98-100, 102-104, 115, fig. 21 Maison au Sud du Temple aux Rhytons	15				6							9	40	
Monchambert 2004														
245–268, figs. 104-111	58			14	10		2			11		21	30	16
Al-Maqdissi and Matoïan 2008														
149-152, figs. 24-29 Royal Palace, Ugarit	5										1	1	13	
Sauvage and Lorre 2023														
80–82, figs. 3-4, no. 76863											1			
93–109, figs. 11-16	18				4	2	1					1	44	1
110–113, figs. 17–18				2			5			1				
267–303, figs. 3-4, Tomb 3	4				1								17	
270–271, Tomb 3	2				2							1	6	
279-287, Tomb 4	1						2						13	
289-303, Tomb 6	4								3			2	1	
307-313, figs. 4-9, Burial 2	19			2	2	2				1	1		3	
316–320, Tomb 5									1				1	
321-335, figs. 17-18, Deposit 213	51	1			1					2		2	2	
339-345, figs. 2, 4, Minet el-Beidha, Dépôts 13–20, 43	3												2	
347-349, figs. 1-2, Egyptian Deposit	1											1	1	4
352-355, fig. 5, Tranchée 8.4													1	
359-364, figs. 5,7, Ras Shamra infant burials				1							1			
365-369, fig. 6, Ras Shamra, Tomb II	4											1	11	
373-376, fig. 3, Ras Shamra, Tomb III	2				1								4	
377-380, fig. 5, Ras Shamra, Tomb IV													2	
381-383, fig. 1, Ras Shamra, Tomb V	1						1						5	
385-389, figs. 1-2, Ras Shamra, Tomb XXXVII	15						5					3	7	
391-400, Ras Shamra, Tomb LIII	17		5	4			3				1	4		
401-412, figs. 2-3, 5-6, Ras Shamra Small Collections	3		2			1	7				1		2	
WARE TOTAL	226	1	26	33	2	6	41	13	16	5	26	54	216	5
GRAND TOTAL	670													

Table 1. *Cypriot pottery excavated at Ugarit and Minet el-Beidha (prepared by Nathan Meyer).*

In *Ugartica* VII, Courtois and Courtois (1978) presented the finds from the 1959-1968 seasons and were much more careful in listing local and imported materials; the Cypriot pottery was no exception. Whilst all Cypriot wares were presented in the same section(s), there was no overall discussion and no concordance of the wares by context. All contexts are provided (e.g., '*Sud Acropole, point top*. 3793', '*Sud Fortresse* – 2.5 m', 'RS 1965, *secteur* 217') but effectively just as in Schaeffer's (1949) earlier publication. Thus, once again, the result is that only a more focused study — in which all the material was presented by context — would enable fuller discussion. In this case, however, one can at least tally the amounts of some Cypriot wares; the majority are listed in Table 1, essentially as the authors presented them.

Courtois and Courtois (1978: 210–211 and fig. 5) also mention without specific numbers the following MC III-LC I wares: 15 examples of Red-on-Black, Monochrome, White Painted Pendant Line Style, Proto-Base-ring (?) and Base-ring I (or Red Slip?). Also listed in this manner are 18 examples of Base-ring I-II, 'Apliki ware', Proto-White Slip (?), White Painted V/VI (Courtois and Courtois 1978: 286–289, fig. 31), as well as 10 miscellaneous examples of Base-ring II (including one bull-shaped rhyton, inv. 24.435), White Slip II, Monochrome and Red-on-Black wares (Courtois and Courtois 1978: 290–291, fig. 32). The 12 vessels (*rhyta, askoi*, kraters) listed in Table 1 under Rude Style are described as 'Style Rude Chypro-Mycenien' (Courtois and Courtois 1978: 324–331, figs. 43, 45).

Regarding such terminology, wares formerly defined as Rude or Pastoral Style, Late Helladic IIIB and IIIC:1b, or Decorated Late Cypriot III are now collectively referred to as White Painted Wheelmade III ware (Åström 1972a: 276; Sherratt 1991: 186–187; Steel 1998: 288; Kling 2000: 281–282; Georgiou 2018b). Recent petrographic analyses of LC IIC Aegean-type painted and unpainted fine wares (White Painted Wheelmade) from Hala Sultan Tekke has reconfirmed the local production (i.e., on Cyprus) of these wares (Waiman-Barak et al. 2023), long since indicated by earlier work (e.g., Anson 1980; Jones and Catling 1986: 603–609; Knapp and Cherry 1994: 50, 61–62; Mountjoy and Mommsen 2015). By the LC IIIA period, such Aegean-type wares became increasingly prominent and appear to have been mass-produced, perhaps in centrally organised workshops at sites such as Enkomi, Hala Sultan Tekke or Kition. Thus, we may define all such vessels from Ugarit as Cypriot in origin.

Regarding the 14 Red Lustrous spindle bottles (listed in Table 1 although their Cypriot origin is questionable), Courtois and Courtois (1978: 256–257, fig. 20) were certainly aware of the controversy over the production centre(s) of Red Lustrous wares. In a two-page aside, they list their most prominent occurrences (Cyprus, Anatolia, northwest Syria) without stating any preference on their origins (on the likely Anatolian origin of this ware, see most recently Kibaroğlu et al. 2019; cf. Knappett 2000; Knappett and Kilikoglu 2007).

Courtois and Courtois (1978: 336–337, fig. 48.2) also mention the fragment of a Mycenaean vessel with a Cypro-Minoan sign. Hirschfeld (2000: 165–166) noted two other 'marked' vessels from the tell at Ras Shamra, one a White Shaved juglet, the other a Base-ring bowl. For the sake of completeness, one may also note that the clay composition of a sample of White Slip wares recovered at both Ugarit and Enkomi was evaluated using Neutron Activation Analysis (NAA) (Artzy et al. 1981): all these wares were found to be a close match to other examples from Enkomi, further demonstrating a Cypriot origin and the close links between these two sites (see also Renson et al. 2013).

In two separate publications, Monchambert (1983, 2004) presented some of the ceramic materials excavated during the 1975-76 excavations at Ugarit. In the first of these, he discussed local imitations of Cypriot wares (Monchambert 1983: 27–29; see now also Vilain 2023) and illustrated the following: flask with handle (1983: 37, fig. 1:5), 2 kraters (1983: 41, fig. 3:14,15), 4 White Slip milk bowls (1983: 39, fig. 2:6-9) and 1 juglet (1983: 39, fig.2:10). In the second work, Monchambert (2004: 245–268, figs. 104-111) listed materials that derived from three areas of excavation in *'secteur A'*: the residential sector, squares A14–I51, and the North Residence along with houses to its south (Monchambert 2004: 12–14, figs. 2–4). Most finds from these years of excavation were of local origin and stemmed exclusively from habitational contexts; the Cypriot imports are listed in Table 1 here (except for one example each of 'Composite Ware' and 'Black Slip IV').

Between the years 1978-1995, excavations in three houses (*Maisons* A, B, E) in the *Centre de la ville* and another nearby (*Maison au Sud du Temple aux Rhytons*) produced, by my count, 85 Cypriot vessels (Yon 1987: 11–123; Yon and Arnaud 2001: 83–190; cf. Bell 2006: 40, table 6, who tallied 98 Cypriot finds from these same excavations). These vessels are comprised mainly of White Slip ware (45 items) and Base-ring bowls, flasks and jugs (18 items); the remainder are Monochrome and White Shaved wares (all listed in Table 1).

In a preliminary publication of some materials excavated in the LBA Royal Palace at Ugarit, Al-Maqdissi and Matoïan (2008) discussed several vessels of local Levantine, Mycenaean and Cypriot manufacture, as well as a MC III-LC I White Painted Pendent Line Style jug from a tomb predating the construction of the palace. Nineteen White Slip, Base-ring and White Shaved wares were presented and illustrated (all in Table 1).

Sauvage (2012: 179–180) mentioned some early Cypriot imports (MC III-LC I) at Ugarit and Minet el-Beidha: White Painted VI (closed forms), Red Slip and Red-on-Black wares (Ugarit—Schaeffer 1949: pl. 130–131 and Tomb 4496; Courtois and Courtois 1978: 203 fig. 2.15, 210–211 fig. 5; Minet el-Beidha—Schaeffer 1949: fig. 51, Burials 1 and 2). Some rare examples of Base-ring I and Monochrome wares from Late Bronze I levels were also noted. Monochrome Wares, Sauvage added, are mainly attested in well-stratified levels of the 13th century BC at Ugarit, e.g., in the House of Urtenu.

Citing Hankey (1967), who first proposed that Cypriot merchants might have served as intermediaries in the transmission of Mycenaean pottery to the Levant, Sauvage (2012: 184) suggested that a large portion of the Mycenaean pottery found at Ugarit likely originated in Cyprus. Similarly, van Wijngaarden (2002: 276–277) argued that the concentration of Mycenaean pottery amongst Levantine urban groups, not least those at Ugarit, reflects commercial exchange between elites in both Cyprus and the Levant. In his view, "… the Levant, at least initially, relied on Cypriot initiative to acquire these [Mycenaean] vessels." During the 13th century BC, furthermore, Mycenaean style pottery (Rude/

Pastoral, Simple) was probably produced on Cyprus, perhaps reflecting a shift in the main node of exchange, from Greece to Cyprus. Alternatively, the Cypriots may have produced these wares themselves, imitating the Aegean products that passed through their ports.

In one of the most recent volumes treating previously unpublished finds from Schaeffer's field expeditions, Sauvage and Lorre (2023) present materials excavated by the French mission at Ras Shamra between 1929-1935. These finds stem mainly from Minet el-Beidha and the authors focus particularly on the contexts and interpretation of collections held in the Musée d'Archéologie Nationale in Saint-Germain-en-Laye (Sauvage and Lorre 2023: 11, 29).

Much of the first part of the volume is taken up with a year-by-year description of the history of discoveries and contains some excellent site and trench plans of both Ugarit and Minet el-Beidha (Sauvage and Lorre 2023: 30–64). Some Cypriot materials are presented here in a rather stark manner: for example, one minor tomb of rubble construction (14th-13th centuries BC?) contained White Slip II, White Shaved and Base-ring wares and one Mycenaean bowl (Sauvage and Lorre 2023: 35-36). Further generalised descriptions of a wide range of contexts (e.g., *chantier*, *muret*, *tranchée*) with other Cypriot material follow. The pottery catalogue itself comes next (Sauvage and Lorre 2023: 71–155): all examples — whether local, other Levantine or Cypriot imports — are presented together and, to tally the Cypriot imports, it was necessary to consult each entry. For example, of 12 vessels listed for the Middle Bronze Age, there is one Cypriot import, of White Painted Pendent Line Style (Sauvage and Lorre 2023: 80–82, figs. 3-4, no. 76863) (Table 1 here lists all examples).

For the LBA, fortunately the Cypriot imports from Ugarit and Minet el-Beidha are collected together in a separate section; some contextual evidence is provided (Sauvage and Lorre 2023: 93–109, figs. 11-16). In addition to a Cypriot wall bracket, the pottery includes the following wares and shapes: White Shaved dipper juglets (*puisettes*); White Slip bowls; Base-ring I and II cups and juglets; Monochrome bowls and (rarely) Plain White, White and Grey/Black Lustrous Wheelmade bowls (for the specific tallies, see Table 1).

The 5 Red Lustrous examples are likely of Anatolian origin; vessels more certain to be Cypriot in origin are the White and Grey/Black Lustrous vessels (Sauvage and Lorre 2023: 110–113, figs. 17–18; see also Sauvage 2022). Twenty-one Bichrome ware examples are all regarded as Syrian in origin (Yon, in Sauvage and Lorre 2023: 139–155, figs. 1-7), although a Cypriot origin for some of these is likely (see, e.g., Artzy et al. 1973; Artzy 2002). One ivory disc with a decorated border is otherwise unattested at Ugarit, but such discs are quite common on Cyprus (9 examples from Enkomi) (Caubet and Poplin, in Sauvage and Lorre 2023: 173, 175–176, figs. 2-3, no. 76792). Amongst metal items are four bronze bowls that could be of either Cypriot or local origin (Gernez, in Sauvage and Lorre 2023: 233, 249 fig. 13, nos. 91247-91250).

Multiple Cypriot imports recovered from a series of tombs excavated at Minet el-Beidha were first published by Sauvage and Lorre (2023: 267–303, figs. 3-4), along with others held in different collections and published in *Ugaritica* II (Schaeffer 1949). Lead isotope analysis was also carried out on some

White Slip 2 and Base-ring wares from Tomb 3 (Renson et al., in Sauvage and Lorre 2023: 417–420).

Burial 2 (in area of Deposit 213—Sauvage and Lorre 2023: 307–313, figs. 4-9) includes 19 Cypriot vessels, as well as one 'imitation' White Painted Wheelmade II juglet. Three bowls are described as 'Cypriot red and grey' examples. Deposit 213 and 213 bis (Sauvage and Lorre 2023: 321–335, figs. 17-18) held a significant array of Cypriot or Cypriot-inspired wares, including undefined Base-ring jars described as 'bilbils' of various varieties. Sauvage (2006: 623, table 1) also listed 3 Red Lustrous vessels and 7 'other Cypriot ceramics?' from Deposit 213 but these are not included in Table 1, as it assumed that the more recent publication is definitive. There is a long discussion on the possible function of this deposit, a large structure perhaps somehow related with artisanal activities (e.g., production of olive oil or more precious oils?), but the lack of stratigraphic information limits any secure interpretation. Deposits 13-20 and 43 at Minet el-Beidha (Sauvage and Lorre 2023: 339–345, figs. 2, 4) contained only Base-ring and White Slip wares, but there was also one alabaster vase in the form of a Cypriot jug (Vilain 2023: fig. 16a illustrates an imitation *calcite* Base-ring jug from Minet el-Beidha, but it's not clear if this is the same vessel). From Ras Shamra, some infant burials found on the acropolis and several tombs (II–V, XXXVII, LIII) contained a wide array of Cypriot pottery wares (Sauvage and Lorre 2023: 359–400) (all listed in Table 1).

Taking an entirely different approach, Vilain (2023) discusses at length some imitations and 'transpositions' (in stone or metal) of various types of Cypriot ceramics found at Ugarit, Minet el-Beidha, Ras ibn-Hani and other north Syrian sites (Tell Kazel, Tell Atchana). These include especially a range of bowls, flasks, jugs and juglets in Base-ring, White Slip and Monochrome ware. Other, more 'exceptional' types, like kraters or zoomorphic vessels, were not copied since, in her view, they were likely destined only for elite consumption. Certain Cypriot imports thus inspired craftspeople in Ugarit and elsewhere to create not only imitations of those wares but also new combinations exhibiting both Cypriot and Levantine features. In Vilain's view, such imitations only appeared when Cypriot pottery had become fully integrated into the daily life of local people. Although Vilain (2023: 41) states that "… the development of imitations and transpositions offers a much more complex and multifaceted picture of cultural interactions in the Eastern Mediterranean during the second millennium BCE," at no point does she discuss the nature of such interactions.

By way of closing this section, I turn to Papasavvas (2023: 53), who noted that the abundant material Schaeffer excavated at Ugarit — listed in excavation records and notebooks, find inventories, plans and drawings, photographs and imprints of cuneiform tablets — has been and continues to be studied by the current director, Valerie Matoïan, and by other French archaeologists "… as part of a major project to revisit and publish these excavations" (among these are Matoïan 2017, 2019, 2021a; Sauvage and Lorre 2023). In the present study, 670 Cypriot pottery vessels have been tallied from various deposits at Ras Shamra, Minet el-Beidha and Ras Ibn Hani. To that number must be added scores more, some of which are mentioned above. In a similar exercise, Bell (2006: 35, table 4) recorded 875 Mycenaean wares (no LH IIIC) at Ugarit, a further 203 from Minet el-Beidha, as well as 16 from

Ras ibn Hani. Such estimates, of course, are far from precise and reveal little about how the various inhabitants of Ugarit or its harbours might have accessed or used these imported goods, not least because the numbers are affected by the size of the excavated contexts (Bell 2006: 31). Nonetheless, they provide at least a good impression of the striking amount of Cypriot ceramic material uncovered over several decades of excavations at Ugarit.

CHAPTER 5

LEVANTINE MATERIAL IN CYPRUS

Although on more solid ground here than is the case with Cypriot material found in Ugarit, Papasavvas (2023) has encapsulated some of the problems in his revealing new study of the history of excavations ('Trench Warfare') at Enkomi (for an alternative view, see Lagarce 1993). Despite such contentious issues, Enkomi is a site whose material remains illustrate well Cyprus's intimate links with the entire Levantine littoral, and especially with Ugarit.

On the positive side, Schaeffer (1936a) corrected earlier excavators' mistaken impressions that the materials above the LBA tombs they were excavating at Enkomi dated to the Byzantine period (Lagarce 1993: 93–94; Papasavvas 2023: 10). Schaeffer demonstrated clearly that the LC tombs and the domestic remains above them were contemporaneous (see also Catling 1983: 72). The French Mission under Schaeffer had been drawn to Enkomi by rich finds of Mycenaean pottery and other distinctive imports, as well as their similarity to material Schaeffer had excavated at Ugarit. Indeed, Schaeffer (1936b: 148; 1971: 520–523) believed the Mycenaeans had established a colony at Ugarit and, following on from his work there, assigned a 14th century BC date to Enkomi's monumental ashlar buildings (Papasavvas 2023: 12).

Papasavvas (2023: 174) stresses that Schaeffer dug primarily to recover significant finds and sought to establish a general historical reconstruction. Between 1929, when he began excavating at Ugarit, and 1948, when he published his opus, *Stratigraphie comparée*, Schaeffer had developed a chronological-historical scheme for several different areas of the ancient Mediterranean and Near East, which he continued to apply elsewhere. When he came to work in the field of Cypriot archaeology (especially after 1946), Schaeffer brought with him these pre-judgements about what he would find and how it should be interpreted.

Schaeffer excavated at Enkomi for over 30 years, exposing multiple structures and retrieving literally thousands of finds. As Antoniadou (2005: 69) once observed, the rapid clearance of large areas aimed at discovering buildings with significant historical information "… proved to be less a productive than a destructive procedure of excavation." Papasavvas (2023: 13) maintains that because all this fieldwork "… was clearly beyond the scope of a single archaeologist.… the French Mission's work has been published only incompletely in a series of volumes and reports" (listing, e.g., Schaeffer 1936a, 1952, 1971; Courtois 1981; Lagarce and Lagarce 1985; Courtois et al. 1986). Papasavvas (2023: 13) concludes: "… these publications are seriously compromised by a lack of close stratigraphic observation, a reliance on a preconceived historical reconstruction and on some chronological misinterpretations" (citing Iacovou 1988; Kling 1989; Webb 2001). Schaeffer's excavations at Enkomi, in other words, reveal a lack of methodological rigour and the selective publication of finds that he considered to be of historical significance for his interpretations (Papasavvas (2023: 115).

The differing fieldwork strategies, mentalities and resulting interpretations of Schaeffer and the Cypriot archaeologist Porphyrios Dikaios concerning the site of Enkomi are documented at length by Papasavvas (2023). Here, it must suffice to say that Schaeffer eventually came around to Dikaios's view that the Mycenaean pottery from Enkomi must be 13th (not 14th) century BC in date, but never acknowledged his debt to the more careful stratigraphic work of his Cypriot colleague (Dikaios 1969-1971).

At this point, it is also necessary to caution that it is seldom possible to define material evidence from Ugarit specifically as opposed to that from the Levantine coast more widely. Craftspeople at Ugarit clearly were capable of producing distinctive goods (Caubet and Yon 2001: 149–150; Matoïan and Vita 2020: 32–33), and such products as well as raw materials (e.g., metals, timber) could have been transhipped via its ports (Kassianidou 2003: 116; Bell 2006: 85–87). Even if finished goods were manufactured mainly for local consumption, Ugarit's role in regional trading spheres was multivariate and multifaceted.

In any case, in order to consider the range of Levantine material on Cyprus, let us take the obvious example of the Canaanite Jar (CJ), arguably the best known, most widely represented Maritime Transport Container (MTC) in the Bronze Age Mediterranean (e.g., Grace 1956; Amiran 1970: 139–142; Parr 1973; Georgiou 2014: 175–176; Knapp and Demesticha 2017: 46–66). Petrographic and chemical analyses of CJ sherds from Kom Rabia (near Memphis in Egypt) revealed four distinctive compositional groups, the most northerly of which was the area around Tell Kazel and Tell Arqa (Ownby and Smith 2011), nearly 150 kms south of Ugarit (see Figure 6b, above). Further petrographic analyses revealed that over 80% of the approximately 150 CJs retrieved from the Uluburun shipwreck were characterised by sediments typical of the region around Tel Abu Hawam and Haifa Bay (a similar origin was assigned to other CJs found in Egypt — Serpico et al. 2003: 373); a second group (14%) stemmed from the area between Tyre and Sidon in Lebanon (Pulak 2008: 317-318, n. 5; Goren 2013: 57). Beyond petrographic studies, other analytical work (Neutron Activation Analysis, Organic Residues Analysis) carried out on LBA CJs indicates a variety of likely contents (e.g., wine, olive oil, pistacia resin) and multiple possible production centres, from the Bay of Haifa all the way north to Syria if not Cilicia (e.g., Serpico et al. 2003; Smith et al. 2004; Killebrew 2007: 175-180; more generally, see Cateloy 2016; Pedrazzi 2016, 2022).

As a result, in what follows my aim once again is to provide an impression rather than a quantitative analysis of Levantine material (i.e., not specifically from Ugarit) found on Cyprus. I begin with Levantine pottery, the most abundant and obvious indicator.

LEVANTINE POTTERY ON CYPRUS

In her prominent corpus of southern Levantine pottery, Amiran (1970: 140) maintained that the CJ was not valued or exchanged because of its intrinsic value but rather for what it contained, most likely oil or wine. Currently, some 350 CJs have been found at 21 different Middle and Late Bronze Age sites on Cyprus (Table 2). One of the most prominent and complete examples stems from a MC III burial (Tomb 1A) at Arpera *Mosphilos* (Merrillees 1974: 44, fig. 29.5, 47, 54 fig. 35) (Figure 8). Crewe (2012: 230–232, fig. 2.1) identified six examples of CJs in MC III-LC I tombs across the island and a further 26 examples in MC III or MC III-LC I settlement contexts at Kalopsidha. Some 84 CJs were recorded at Maa *Palaeokastro* (Hadjicosti 1988), and at least 70 examples are known from the renewed excavations at Pyla *Kokkinokremos* (Georgiou 2014: 176, 186; Bretschneider et al. 2023: 177–178, fig. 6.3.25, and *passim*; Kostopoulou 2024:

Enkomi [at least 20 from the 'Sanctuary of the Ingot god'] [at least 31 total]	Dikaios 1969-71, Volume IIIa: pls. 65:10, 77:22-23; 120:11-12; 125:4; Courtois 1971: 248 fig. 89, 249, 251 fig. 91, 256 fig. 96; 1981: 37-38, fig. 15.3; Gunneweg et al. 1987; Mazar 1988; Åström 1991a; Crewe 2012: 232-234 (minimum count 31)
Arpera *Mosphilos*	Merrillees 1974: 54 fig. 35, 59
Hala Sultan Tekke *Vyzakia* [at least 50 vessels]	Åström et al. 1976: 15-16, pl. XVd; Åström 1991b; Fischer 1991; Åström 1989: 118; Fischer and Bürge 2018: 224-225, fig. 3.16 (8 examples)
Alassa *Pano Mandilares* and *Paleotaverna* [8 fragments]	Hadjisavvas 2017: 412-414
Kalopsidha 'C', 'Gjerstad's house' [at least 26 examples]	Åström 1966: 9; Crewe 2010: 68; 2012: 230-232, fig. 2.1
Pyla *Verghi* [at least 5 vessels]	Grace 1956: 92 n. 22; Åström 1972a: 261; Cydrisse Cateloy, pers. comm., October 2023
Korovia *Nitovikla*	Crewe 2012: 232 ('significant quantities')
Galinoporni Tomb 1(?)	Crewe 2012: 230-231, fig. 2.5
Pyla *Kokkinokremos* [at least 70 vessels]	Karageorghis and Demas 1984: 51, pls. 37-38; Georgiou 2014: 176, 186; Bretschneider et al. 2023: 177–178, fig. 6.3.25, and *passim*
Kition	Karageorghis and Demas 1985: 279
Kition *Bamboula* [at least 117 vessels]	Georgiou et al. 2022-23
Kouklia *Palaepaphos*	Maier and Karageorghis 1984: 54
Kouklia *Evreti* [at least 33]	Jacobs 2016: 44-45, 50 fig.21, 66-68
Kouklia *Kaminia* [Tomb VII: 1]	Jones and Catling 1986: 572, pl. 7.16
Kouklia *Eliomylia* [1 complete vessel]	Karageorghis 1990: 79 (no.1), 83, pls.85-86
Kouklia *Teratsoudhia* [13 handles]	Karageorghis 1990: 37 (nos.17-18), 38 (no.59), 46 (no.116), 47 (nos.162, 167, 169, 174, 180), 48 (no.200), 50 (nos.41, 55), 53 (no.58)
Maa *Palaeokastro* [84 vessels]	Hadjicosti 1988: 340-385
Maroni *Vournes*, *Tsaroukkas* [at least 6, and 1 in Tomb 15] [+MNI 8 from 2017-19 excavations; 225 sherds]	Cadogan et al. 2001: 77; Manning et al. 2002: 137-140; Manning et al. 2006: 473 table 1, 478 table 2; Atkins 2022: 302; Artemis Georgiou, pers. comm., October 2023
Apliki *Karamallos* [8 fragments from 5 contexts; minimum 5 vessels]	Du Plat Taylor 1952: 160-161 figs. 11.9, 12.4; Kling and Muhly 2007: 149-150, 183
Kalavasos village	Pearlman 1985: 167 fig. 2:1, 168 no. 1
Kalavasos *Ayios Dhimitrios* [11 examples catalogued; 1224 sherds in database]	South et al. 1989: 10, 107, 146, fig. 14, pl. 5:1070-1074; South 1983: 97, 109, pl. 15:3; South 1991: 135 fig. 2 (K-AD 1500); South 1997: 159, pl. 13:2; South 2008: 310, chart pl.63; Alison South, pers. comm., October 2016
Arediou *Vouppes* [161 sherds from 5 different contexts; minimum 5 vessels	Steel and Thomas 2008: 241, fig. 23; Steel and McCartney 2008: 14 table 1, 21; Steel 2022: 91-92, fig. 4.5(2-3); Steel 2023: 197-200, table 4
Myrtou *Pigadhes* ['Syrian jars']	Catling, in du Plat Taylor 1957: 53-55, fig. 23: 318-320).

Table 2. *Canaanite Jars from Cyprus.*

Figure 8. *Canaanite jar from Arpera Mosphilos (Merrillees 1974: 44, fig. 29.5). Courtesy of the Director, Department of Antiquities, Cyprus.*

224). Like earlier work at Hala Sultan Tekke *Vyzakia* (Åström 1991b), the ongoing Swedish excavations at the site continue to turn up more CJs (e.g., Fischer and Bürge 2018: 224–225, fig. 3.16).

Twenty-six of the 84 examples found at Maa *Palaeokastro* were analysed petrographically and chemically (Jones and Vaughan 1988: 393): seven may have been produced on Cyprus. Georgiou (2014: 176, 186; 2024: 264–265, fig. 15.7) also suggested that some CJs from Pyla *Kokkinokremos* may have been local products. Three CJ fragments from Hala Sultan Tekke analysed by petrographic and lead isotope analyses might also represent local production (Renson et al. 2014). Based on NAA of a sample of 19 CJs from Enkomi, Pyla *Kokkinokremos* and Maa *Palaeokastro*, Jung et al. (2023: 191–192) concluded that none were manufactured on Cyprus, at least between the 13th through 11th centuries BC; thus, they regard those CJs as the "… archaeological correlates *par excellence* for goods exchange between Cyprus and the Levant." Nonetheless, the possible instances of locally produced CJs mean that the approximately 350 examples known from the island may not all be imports. In a passing but relevant comment, Sherratt (1998:

300–301 n. 15, 305) noted that some of the oil from pressing installations known at various LC sites (e.g., Kalavasos *Ayios Dhimitrios*, Alassa *Pano Mandilares*, Maroni *Vournes*) may have been exported in locally-made vessels.

Georgiou et al. (2022-23: 137–138, 143) assess and discuss the number of CJs, Egyptian Jars and Cretan Transport Stirrup Jars (TSJs) from Sondage 10 at the site of Kition *Bamboula*. Of three *in situ* residential strata excavated, our concern here is with those dated to the late 13th through 12th centuries BC: LC IIC (Level V.2), LC IIIA (Level V.1) and LC IIIB–Cypro-Geometric (CG) I (Level IV.2). Two sets of numbers are provided, the fragments and the minimum number of individual examples (MNI, based on rim counts). The MNI of CJs (all varied morphologies of the 'bellied' category) recovered at *Bamboula* currently amounts to 117: Level V.2: 39; Level V.1: 32; Level IV.2: 46. It may also be noted that the number of CJs, whether fragments or MNIs, far exceeds the number of Egyptian Jars and TSJs (Georgiou et al. 2022-23: 137). This exemplary paper illustrates well the potential of a quantitative approach.

Some CJs from *Bamboula* bear simple, generic, incised post-firing marks, but one example from Level V.1 seems to correspond to a sign (CM041) of the Cypro-Minoan script (Georgiou et al. 2022-23: 137, n.98). The practice of marking pottery, especially MTCs, was quite common on Cyprus, and has been argued to represent the involvement of Cypriot merchants or their agents in the distribution of such vessels in the eastern Mediterranean, whether from the Levant to Cyprus, or vice-versa (e.g., Hirschfeld 2000: 183–184, 2009; Knapp and Demesticha 2017: 56, 85–86; Donnelly 2022; Knapp and Meyer 2023: 313; Georgiou 2024: 260–261).

Other examples of Levantine pottery found on Cyprus include some Syrian Red and Black Burnished and Plain wares from MC III mortuary deposits at Lapithos and Nicosia *Ayia Paraskevi* (Åström 1972b: 132–133, 240–241; G. Georgiou 2009; on the Burnished wares, see Nigro 2003: 351–354, figs. 11-15). Gjerstad (1926: 269) recorded 'great quantities of Syrian ware' during MC III at Kalopsidha. Crewe's (2007: 51–52) reassessment of the pottery from 'Gjerstad's house' at Kalopsidha, however, indicates this notion should be tempered and the quantities scaled down to some Syro-Palestinian juglets and Tell el-Yahudiyeh ware; notably, the 'house' continued in use during LC IA. Crewe (2012) has argued that, during LC I, people living in eastern Cyprus and along the Karpass peninsula adopted Levantine-style pottery and the technology of wheelmade pottery (e.g., kraters, large jugs) to emulate foreign drinking and food consumption practices — perhaps those of merchants. Levantine dipper juglets and other, similar vessels, ostensibly used to transport (precious?) liquids, are well attested at several MC III-LC I sites (Bushnell 2016: 55-57, 65, 91). Porta and Cannavò (2024: 246–250 fig. 14.10) report on petrographic analysis of a fragmentary *pithos* from LC IIC Pyla *Kokkinokremos*, suggesting an origin somewhere along the southern Levantine coast. The same authors point to two further *pithoi* from Kition that also appear to be of Levantine origin (Porta and Cannavò 2024: 249–250, citing examples from Xenophontos et al. 2000). Steel (2022: 90-92, fig. 4.5.1) mentioned two joining sherds of a Levantine string-cut platter bowl and the flat base of another from LC IIC Aredhiou *Vouppes*; such bowls are uncommon on Cyprus.

By contrast, finds of what were once regarded as 'Palestinian' Bichrome ware on Cypriot sites are extensive; however, because many have been shown to be of local manufacture, they are difficult to quantify accurately. Åström's (2001: 136–141) attempt calculated 76 handmade examples from 13 sites, and 241 wheelmade examples from 38 sites (including 700 sherds from Nitovikla); Enkomi and Hala Sultan Tekke had over 50 examples each. From the renewed excavations at Hala Sultan Tekke, Bürge (in Fischer and Bürge 2018: 254) discussed both plain and Bichrome-decorated flasks; in her view, judging from macroscopic examination of the fabric and preliminary petrographic analyses, "… all of them are likely Levantine imports." Such conclusions, however, seem at best premature.

Based on Epstein's (1966) early monograph on Bichrome ware found throughout southern Anatolia, the Levant, Egypt and Cyprus, its origin was regarded to be somewhere in the northern Levant, with a timespan dated mainly to the 16th-15th centuries BC. Following analytical work employing NAA, however, a team from the Lawrence Berkeley Laboratory argued for the Cypriot provenance of Bichrome wheelmade wares found on the island as well as some others found on Levantine sites (e.g., Artzy 1973; Artzy et al. 1973, 1975). Although opinions on their origin persist (e.g., compare Artzy 2001a and Karageorghis 2001), and even though some of the Bichrome wheelmade ware found on Cyprus might well be of Levantine origin, until more definitive provenance studies (e.g., NAA and more detailed petrographic analyses) are carried out (Kostopoulou and Jung, in Bretschneider et al. 2023: 255; Riehle et al. 2023), this ware should be considered to be primarily of Cypriot origin (no Bichrome ware found at Ugarit was included in Table 1, above).

A somewhat similar problem exists regarding Tell el-Yahudiyeh (TEY) ware found on Cyprus. Because many TEY vessels date to the Middle Bronze II period (Negbi 1978), they are not directly relevant to this study. However, given that the literature on TEY ware is immense and ever expanding, the following offers a tentative overview of a very complex situation.

Based on finds from the potter's kiln excavated at 'Afula in Israel, Amiran (1970: 120) argued that TEY ware was manufactured in the Levant and exported to Cyprus and Egypt. Kaplan (1980), however, argued that TEY ware was first produced in Egypt and that the earliest examples found in the Levant (MB IIA-B) originated in Egypt. Based on a meticulous study of TEY wares from Tell ed-Dab'a in the Egyptian Delta, Aston (2008: 190) clarified that there were two main branches of development in these wares, a Palestinian group and a Levanto-Egyptian group, but noted that a third, handmade group (Egyptian) possibly owed its origins to Cypriot Black Slip II wares (see also Aston and Bietak 2012). Given such differences of opinion, subsequent studies often turned to chemical or petrographic analyses of TEY ware, most of which point to production centres in Egypt or the Levant.

For our purposes, the most significant study was Artzy and Asaro's (1979) chemical analyses (NAA, XRF) of 29 TEY jugs, juglets and sherds — 21 from Cyprus and 8 from the potter's kiln at 'Afula in Israel (for which see Zevulin 1990). Of the Cypriot examples, 8 most likely originated in the Nile Delta, 8 further examples probably came from Egypt, and the remaining 5 could be of Egyptian origin. None of the Cypriot examples were consistent with the then-known chemical composition groups of Levantine and Cypriot pottery (Artzy and Asaro 1979: 139–140). Although the authors concluded that the later (MB IIB-C) examples of TEY ware thus seem to have produced in Egypt, earlier (MB IIA) examples might have originated in the Levant.

There is no shortage of further analytical work on TEY wares suggesting Levantine origins. Although Kaplan (1980), for example, analysed four TEY vessels from Ras Shamra and assigned them to a minor chemical group of the same name, more recent studies suggest that these vessels derived from Egypt or the southern Levant (Aston and Bietak 2012: 142; cf. Shammas 2023: 147). Griffiths (2011-12) conducted optical microscopy analysis on the fabric of 20 TEY juglets excavated in Middle Bronze Age contexts at Sidon, Lebanon; the petrographic features of all but one of these juglets indicated production on Lebanon's coastal plain. The same origin was proposed based on fabric analyses of selected examples of TEY ware from Tel Kabri in Israel (Goren and Cohen-Weinberger 2002: 441–442). Petrographic analysis of 22 Middle Bronze II TEY ware samples from Tell Arqa in Lebanon likewise indicated multiple possible manufacturing locations along the Levantine coast, from north to south (Ownby, in Aston and Bietak 2012: 607–608).

The most recent classification of TEY wares concludes that there were multiple production centres and workshops in the northern Levant and argues that there were two separate lines of TEY ware development: (1) Levanto-Egyptian and (2) Syro-Palestinian (Shammas 2023: 146–149, 160–162). By contrast, Aston and Bietak's (2012) massive study, focused firmly on the classification and chronology of TEY wares recovered at Tell el-Dab'a in the Egyptian delta, seems to indicate that most of these wares, including those found on Cyprus, were produced in Egypt, not in the Levant.

Turning specifically to Cyprus, Åström (1957: 239) long ago observed that TEY ware was 'in vogue' on Cyprus only for a short time during the MC III-LC I period. In his view, an early style of TEY ware decorated with panels of punctured triangles is 'reflected' in Black Slip III ware, which dates to the end of the MC III period. Bushnell (2016: 63–64, table 25, fig. 42) listed 87 examples of TEY juglets from Cyprus but maintained that it is difficult to distinguish between imports and local Cypriot imitations. Merrillees, who has long studied TEY wares (and what he saw as an earlier variant, 'el-Lisht' wares) (e.g., Merrillees 1974: 43–77; 1978), felt that all TEY juglets of the Levanto-Egyptian group — the most numerous representatives of this ware on the island — originated in Egypt (Merrilllees 2007: 90–91).

Earlier examples of the Levanto-Egyptian group — e.g., three piriform juglets from Arpera *Mosphilos* Tomb 1 and three from Morphou *Toumba tou Skourou* Tomb V — were, in his view, less straightforward but he concluded nonetheless that "… the data point strongly to an Egyptian source for all the Syro-Egyptian [Levanto-Egyptian] specimens of Tell el-Yahudiyeh Ware found in Cyprus" (Merrillees 2007: 92).

To summarise a complex and obviously still unresolved situation, at least concerning those TEY wares found on Cyprus: their close stylistic links with Black Slip II/III wares suggest that many of the earliest examples at least — i.e., those from

Morphou and Arpera in the island's northwest — may be locally-made imitations. By contrast, the later examples, i.e., those from Enkomi, seem to be Egyptian imports. However, without further elemental (e.g., NAA) or petrographic analyses (as argued by Riehle et al. 2023), it is difficult to assign a specifically Levantine provenance to any of the TEY wares found on the island.

Overall, this discussion of Levantine pottery found on Cyprus — as was the case above in presenting the Cypriot material found in Ugarit — should be regarded as indicative rather than quantitative, even if here stemming from different constraints.

OTHER LEVANTINE MATERIAL ON CYPRUS

Already during the MC and no later than the beginning of LC I (ca. 1650-1600 BC), some people from Cyprus had begun to import and use a range of Levantine goods (Courtois 1986: 71–83), including pottery (G. Georgiou 2009). Others chose to display distinctive types of bronze tools and weapons such as notched chisel axes ('socketed axeheads') and 'warrior belts' (Courtois 1986: 73–75). Such bronzes have been found in mortuary contexts at various Cypriot sites including Dhali *Kafkallia*, Politiko *Chomazoudhia*, Nicosia *Ayia Paraskevi*, Ayios Iakovos *Melia*, Klavdhia *Trimithios* and Kazaphani *Ayios Andronikos* (Overbeck and Swiny 1972: 7–24; Masson 1976: 153–157; Keswani 2004: 80, 121–124) (for location of the sites, see Figure 6a, above). In the Levant, Egypt and Anatolia, bronzes of this type have been recovered from burials not only at Ugarit but also in Jerusalem, Jericho, Tell el-Far'ah North, Tell ed-Dab'a and Kültepe. Even if some of these bronzes were produced on Cyprus, they were clearly inspired by Levantine or Near Eastern prototypes (Philip 1991: 78–83). Equid burials from Politiko *Chomazoudhia* Tomb 3, Kalopsidha Tomb 9 and Lapithos Tomb 322B also seem to reflect Levantine and Near Eastern ideas or ideologies (Buchholz 1973; Courtois 1986: 74; Keswani 2004: 80). Steel (2013: 148–152) perceptively regarded these warrior burials and the goods associated with them — bronze axes, warrior belts, equid burials — as material indicators of increasing Cypro-Levantine mercantile contacts and the appropriation by emerging Cypriot elites of Near Eastern symbols and ideologies of power and status.

Crewe's (2010: 68) study of several Levantine- or Syrian-inspired pottery vessels from MC III-LC I Kalopsidha led her to suggest that the site enjoyed "privileged access to imported goods and trade relations." Amongst other imports and luxury objects dated to the LC I era are Syrian and Old Babylonian cylinder seals, worked bone and ivory, ostrich eggs, gold jewellery and other precious metal objects, semi-precious stones and faience ornaments (see, e.g., Courtois 1986: 83–84; Peltenburg 1995; Keswani 2004: 136; Fischer and Bürge 2022: 23–25, fig. 9).

During the LC II era (14th-13th centuries BC), Cypriot élites — and amongst them certainly merchants — imported Levantine ivory, gold, faience and ceramic objects (Keswani 1989: 69–70), as well as cylinder seals if not weights (Courtois 1986: 85–86). Although many of these imports are dated to the LC IIC or LC IIIA periods, some certainly had antecedents from early in the LC II period, about 1450 BC. The ceremonial display evident at LC IIA Ayios Iakovos *Dhima*, for example, included a bronze lion figurine and a glass juglet of Base-ring shape, both likely Levantine imports (Webb 1999: 31–33 and fig. 7.7; Steel 2013: 154–155). Earlier imports are also evident at sites such as Alassa *Paleotaverna*, Kalavasos *Ayios Dhimitrios*, Hala Sultan Tekke *Vyzakia* and Pyla *Kokkinokremos* (summarised with references in Knapp 1994: 282–90; see more recently Fischer and Bürge 2018: 463–476; Bretschneider et al. 2021: 625–627, figs. 14–16; Bretschneider et al. 2023: figs. 3.17, 3.32, 4.13, 4.87, 5.16, 5.95, and discussions *passim*).

From a LC IIIA (early 12th century BC) context at Hala Sultan Tekke came a silver bowl inscribed in Ugaritic cuneiform (Åström 1986: 11–13, figs. 11–14). Although this type of bowl is well known from LBA-early Iron Age contexts in both Cyprus and the Levant, the closest parallels for this particular bowl come from Megiddo (Åström and Masson 1982: 72 n.5). The short inscription reads: 'Aky, son of Yiptahaddu, made [this] bowl'; *Aky* is a Hurrian name and *Yiptahaddu* is Semitic (Åström and Masson 1982: 75; Bordreuil 1983). *Aky* is also the name used for the site of Akko (Haifa Bay), e.g. in a text from Ras Shamra (RS 18.031) to indicate where a ship from Tyre was undergoing repair (Monroe 2009: 98).

Faience vessels imported from the Levant or possibly from Egypt appear widely in both mortuary and habitational contexts on Cyprus (Peltenburg 2002). Concentrations of faience vessels have been found in Kition Tomb 9, Enkomi British Tomb 66, and Tombs 1 and 9 at Kition *Chrysopolitissa* (Peltenburg 1974: 105–144). From Enkomi, several LC IIC tombs contained faience and other Levantine luxury goods such as glass and ivory (French Tomb 5, Swedish Tomb 11, Cypriot Tomb 10). Swedish Tomb 18 contained the most elaborate collection of ivories, including a comb and other toilet articles. Other prominent luxury items found in Enkomi tombs and dated to the very end of LC IIC (around 1200 BC) include elaborately carved ivory *pyxides* (British Tombs 24, 75), mirror standards (British Tombs 16, 17, 33) and an ivory gaming board depicting a figure wearing a feather-like headdress (British Tomb 58). The iconography of these ivories distinguishes them from other mortuary goods; they portray scenes that arguably symbolise Levantine and Near Eastern elite ideologies (Lagarce and Lagarce 1986: 137; Keswani 1989: 68).

Feldman (2006) presented what she termed 'International Style' ivory, gold, faience and alabaster items from Ugarit that would have enhanced the status of (mercantile) élites, both in the Levant and on Cyprus. She noted that some ivory and faience objects from Cyprus depict themes or compositions like those of certain prestige goods found in Ugarit (Feldman 2006: 10-11, 30-31). The striking LC IIC faience conical rhyton from Kition *Chrysopolitissa*, for example, is decorated with a combination of Levantine, Egyptian and Aegean motifs (Peltenburg 1974: 116–126, pl. XCIV), whilst the well-known ivory box from British Tomb 58 at Enkomi (LC IIIA) depicts various horned and hoofed animals fleeing before a chariot holding an archer, as well as a large bull with lowered horns facing the chariot (Murray et al. 1900: 12–14, pl. I). Feldman (2006: 65 and pl. 8) compared the bull and a hunter spearing a charging lion on this ivory box with similar features on a gold plate from Ugarit. Thus, this object portrays direct iconographic links to luxury items from Ugarit (see also Caubet 2009; Feldman and Sauvage 2010: 73–79). That items such as this gold plate were fashioned in

Ugarit seems highly likely, based on various streams of evidence, if not actual metal workshops (Matoïan 2018; Matoïan and Vita 2020). Finally, Caubet and Yon (2001) discussed the various 'treasures of Ugarit' excavated over many seasons (statuettes, small finds and jewellery in metal, precious stones and faience), emphasizing the "close relations that linked Cyprus (*Alašiya*) and Ugarit at the end of the Late Bronze" (Caubet and Yon 2001: 149).

This list could be extended at length, with respect to both artefacts and iconography (see, for example, Keswani 2004: 84–144, 154–160; Caubet 2009; Feldman and Sauvage 2010: 140–144; Catling 2020: 184–194; Fischer and Bürge 2021, 2022). Moreover, raw materials like ivory had to be imported, most likely from the Levant, and ivory workshops seem to be attested at both Ugarit (Caubet and Poplin 1992) and Kouklia *Evreti* (von Rüden 2016: 340–345). The intention here, however, is to indicate through some selected examples the widespread presence on Cyprus of objects imported from Ugarit or the wider Levant, as well as some other, prestige goods closely linked stylistically to similar items of Levantine or Ugaritic origin. As Yon (2003: 45) noted, we may also assume that ships arriving from the Levant carried other, perishable materials such as food, clothing, grains or animal products that left no trace in the material record (for other organic goods likely exchanged, see Knapp 1991: 35–41).

CHAPTER 6

Cyprus and Ugarit: Documentary Evidence

The documentary evidence from Ugarit involves mainly two scripts: (1) Akkadian (logosyllabic) cuneiform, the one first attested at the site, and (2) alphabetic (or Ugaritic) cuneiform, at least partly based on Akkadian cuneiform but especially on the alphabetic writing systems emerging elsewhere in the Levant at that time (see, e.g., Sass 2017; Boyes 2021: 10–16; Höflmayer et al. 2021; Richey 2023). Alphabetic cuneiform was used primarily to express Ugaritic, the local west Semitic language closely related to other Canaanite dialects used in the Levant. In general, Akkadian was employed at Ugarit mainly for diplomatic and other international correspondence as well as legal texts, whilst Ugaritic was adopted largely for use in internal correspondence and administrative matters, and for writing literary, mythological and religious texts (Boyes 2021: 16).

In the following, thematic sections, both Akkadian and Ugaritic documents are presented together to enable a comprehensive presentation of all the evidence. All relevant information for each text — registration number, findspot (where known), topic, original reference — is presented in Tables 3–4.

PEOPLE, POLITICS AND PROFESSIONS

PEOPLE
Most of the following inventories, lists of personal names or personnel, ration and provision lists, and ritual texts indicate that Cypriots — broadly speaking — of multiple professions participated in diverse activities within the town or palace at Ugarit. Craftspeople, builders, foreign messengers and rulers, soldiers, elderly people and religious personnel received rations of food or wine, if not payments in some agreed upon standard. Whatever their ultimate meaning may be, ritual texts and some letters — like Ugaritic text RS 18.113A (see below, under *Professions*) —

Ugaritic: Text nos.	Findspot	Subject	References
KTU 1.40–RS 1929.2	Ugarit	ritual listing foreign rulers, including 'chief' of Alašiya ('ulp Alty)	Xella 1981: 256-257
KTU 1.41–RS 61/24.325	Ugarit	liver model mentioning Aldy (the Alašiyan?)	Dietrich & Loretz 1969: 173-174
KTU 1.84–RS 17.100	Ugarit	ritual (?) text with titles including 'ulp Alty ('chief' of Alašiya)	Herdner 1963: 134-136
KTU 2.42+2.43–RS 18.113A+B	Ugarit-palace room 77	Alašiyan merchant at Ugarit to buy ships	Virolleaud 1965: 14-15; Knapp 1983
KTU 2.46–RS 18.147		Pgn to king of Ugarit;'akl (food) sent [to Alašiya?]	Virolleaud 1965: 87-88
KTU 2.47–RS 18.148	Ugarit-palace (tablet kiln)	Yadinu requests 150 ships	Virolleaud 1965: 88-89
KTU 4.81–RS 11.779	Ugarit-palace	'catalogue of ships' in Maḫadu, with captains	Herdner 1963: 173-74; Linder 1981: 40
KTU 4.93–RS 11.800+ 11.776	Ugarit	Administrative list of 'old ones' including bn.alṯn	Virolleaud 1941: 17-19
KTU 4.102–RS 11.857	Ugarit-palace entrance	census list including those of Alašiyan families/ households	Herdner 1963: 168-169; Virolleaud 1940: 267-273
KTU 4.149–RS 15.39	Ugarit-palace east archive	list of wine provisions including an Alašiyan	Virolleaud 1957: 114-115; Monroe 2016: 83
KTU 4.155–RS 15.51		list of craftsmen including gentilic [a]lty–'of Alašiya'	Virolleaud 1957: 62-63
KTU 4.175–RS 15.96		list of provisions including a female Alašiyan	Virolleaud 1957: 128
KTU 4.232–RS 16.355		list of names including patronymic bn.alṯn	Virolleaud 1957: 72-73
KTU 4.263–RS 17.49	Ugarit-palace east archive	list of mkrm (merchants)	Virolleaud 1957: 84
KTU 4.337– RS 18.24	Ugarit-palace (tablet kiln)	delivery of copper and tin to Bi'ruti (Ras Ibn Hani?)	Virolleaud 1965: 124-126
KTU 4.343–RS 18.29		personnel list including 'Alty as part of a name	Virolleaud 1965: 107
KTU 4.352–RS 18.42	Ugarit-palace (tablet kiln)	660 measures of oil for Abiramu the Alašiyan	Virolleaud 1965: 117-118
KTU 4.390–RS 18.119	Ugarit-palace	Inventory of ship from Alašiya in 'Atlg	Virolleaud 1965: 74; Knapp 1983
KTU 4.394–RS 18.132	Ugarit-palace (tablet kiln)	copper cargo lost at sea	Virolleaud 1965: 110
KTU 4.609–RS 19.16		ration list for royal personnel, including Aldy	Virolleaud 1965: 18-21
KTU 4.808–RS 94.2392+ 94.2400	Ugarit-House of Urtenu	measures of oil for the Alašiyan	Bordreuil+Pardee 2004: 276–277; Pardee 2023: 95
RS 94.2401	Ugarit-House of Urtenu	Copper and tin for making karkubbûma	Bordreuil 2007: 96-98
RS 24.274	Ugarit	Hurrian-language text in Ugaritic mentioning the 'god of Alašiya'	Laroche 1968: 504-507

Table 3. *Ugaritic Texts treating Cyprus* (Alašiya) *and Ugarit.*
KTU: Dietrich, M., O. Loretz and J. Sanmartín, 2013. Die keilalphabetischen Texte aus Ugarit, Ras Ibn Hani und anderen Orten. *3rd ed. Alter Orient und Altes Testament 360.1. Münster: Ugarit Verlag.*

Akkadian: Text nos.	Findspot	Subject	References
RS 16.126B+257+258	Ugarit	merchant representatives	Nougayrol 1955: 199-203
RS 16.238+254	Ugarit palace	Sinaranu: tax-free goods from *Kabduri* (Crete)	Nougayrol 1955: 107-108
RS 16.386	Ugarit palace	two Ugaritic merchants granted tax-free status	Nougayrol 1955: 165-166
RS 17.35	Ugarit	Tudhaliya verdict: Queen exiles 2 sons to *Alašiya*	Nougayrol 1956: 123
RS 17.146	Ugarit	royal merchants	Nougayrol 1956: 154-157
RS 17.352	Ugarit	Ini-Tešub verdict: Queen exiles 2 sons to *Alašiya*	Nougayrol 1956: 121-122
RS 17.465	Ugarit, Rašap-abu archive	'harbour master'	Nougayrol *et al*. 1968: 20-21, no. 13
RS 18.114		2 brothers flee *Alašiya* to Carchemish via Hatti	Nougayrol 1956: 108
RS 20.18		letter from Ešurwara (*rābiṣu*) to king of Ugarit	Nougayrol et al. 1968: 83-85
RS 20.168	Ugarit–House of Rapanu	King of Ugarit to king of *Alašiya*–oil shipment	Nougayrol et al. 1968: 80-83
RS 20.212	Ugarit	large boat + crew to ship grain to Ura in Cilicia	Nougayrol *et al*. 1968: 105-107
RS 20.238	Ugarit	Ugarit and *Alašiya*; navy of Ugarit in *Lukka* land	Nougayrol *et al*. 1968: 87-89
RS 26.158	Ugarit	boats, grain to Ura	Nougayrol *et al*. 1968: 323-324
RS 34.129	Ugarit-bibliothèque au sud de la ville	Šikila-people 'who live on ships'	Bordreuil 1991: 38-39
RS 34.153	Ugarit-bibliothèque au sud de la ville	horses for *Alašiya* messenger; transhipment of copper to Emar	Bordreuil 1991: 75-76
RS 94.2169	Ugarit–House of Urtenu	'enemy' forces stationed at *Ra'šu* (Ras ibn Hani?)	Lackenbacher & Malbran-Labat 2016: 33-35
RS 94.2173	Ugarit–House of Urtenu	Šinaš (*rābiṣu* of *Alašiya*) + king of Ugarit	Lackenbacher & Malbran-Labat 2016: 41-42
RS 94.2177+2491	Ugarit–House of Urtenu	scribe from Ugarit in royal court of *Alašiya*	Lackenbacher & Malbran-Labat 2016: 38-39
RS 94.2447+2588+2590	Ugarit–House of Urtenu	Šangiwa (*rābiṣu* of *Alašiya*) + king of Ugarit	Lackenbacher & Malbran-Labat 2016: 42-44
RS 94.2475	Ugarit–House of Urtenu	*Kušmešuša* of *Alašiya* sends 33 cu ingots to Niqmaddu of Ugarit	Lackenbacher & Malbran-Labat 2016: 40-41
RS 94.2523, RS 94.2530	Ugarit–House of Urtenu	King of Ugarit fails to send ships to *Lukka*	Lackenbacher & Malbran-Labat 2016: 25-30
RS 94.2561	Ugarit–House of Urtenu	Kinniki (*Alašiya sākinu*) to 'Uzzīnu of Ugarit on mercantile matters	Lackenbacher & Malbran-Labat 2016: 152-154; Pardee (2023) 80
RSL 1		letter to king of Ugarit warning of 'enemy ships'	Nougayrol et al. 1968: 85-86, no. 23

Table 4. *Akkadian Texts treating Cyprus* (Alašiya) *and Ugarit.*

indicate that the people and divinities of Cyprus were somehow involved or invoked in various aspects of ceremonial life at Ugarit.

A census list (KTU 4.102) of the 14th-13th centuries BC documents 30 households with their inhabitants (Walls in Knapp 1996b: 40). The personal names in this list reveal Hurrian, Semitic and Anatolian elements. Although the text itself is written in Ugaritic cuneiform, an Akkadian colophon on the side of the tablet reads ᵁᴿᵁ*Alašiya* (literally, ᵗᵒʷⁿCyprus). The text may refer either to people from *Alašiya* living in Ugarit, or to people from Ugarit living in *Alašiya*.

Several other individuals who either came from *Alašiya*, or else are named after that island (*Aldy* or *Alty*), are mentioned in Ugaritic ration and provision lists, inventories or lists of personal names from Ugarit. For example: KTU 4.609 is a ration list for royal personnel, one of whom — perhaps a joiner — is named *Aldy*, i.e., the *Alašiyan*. In another list of provisions or rations (KTU 4.175), measured by the pot (*dd*), one of the recipients is a woman from *Alašiya*, along with her female apprentices. A fragmentary list of craftspeople (KTU 4.155) may include someone with the gentilic *['a]lty* ('of *Alašiya*') but the name itself is broken off.

Several different people or groups of people were recipients of various quantities of wine. KTU 4.149 is an Ugaritic text that records a list of provisions — mainly pitchers of wine — to be distributed amongst Hittites, Hurrians and the local *maryannu*; two pitchers (of *mth*) were given to the *Alašiyan*. Matoïan and Vita (2018: 311–313) suggested that the recipients might all be foreign diplomats or merchants returning home with wine rations provided for their journey (see Monroe 2022 for a discussion of vineyards in texts from Ugarit). KTU 4.93 is an Ugaritic administrative text entitled 'list of the elders' (*spr ytnm*). This document names at least 56 individuals who were to receive from one to four jars of wine; amongst them was *bn.'altn* ('son of the *Alašiyan*'), who received four jars. Although it must be acknowledged that the specific role or function of those who received deliveries of wine is unclear, they seem to have had various professions — merchants, messengers, soldiers — and are made up of both locals and foreigners.

Divination or ritual texts mentioning people from *Alašiya* are less straightforward. Found during the earliest excavations at Ugarit, KTU 1.40 seems to be a royal ritual listing foreign leaders, including the 'chief' or 'prince' of *Alašiya* (*'ulp Alty*) (Walls in Knapp 1996b: 39, with further refs). This appears to be an expiations sacrifice involving both male and female participants. Although badly damaged and thus difficult to understand, perhaps it was intended to protect people in Ugarit from divine wrath, as personified by various foreigners including the chiefs of the Hurrians, Hittites and *Alašiyans*. Another, very fragmentary ritual text (KTU 1.84) contains the same sequence of titles (including *'ulp Alty*) as the previous one. Such a ritual might suggest that certain people in Ugarit viewed Cyprus as a potentially hostile power. If so, this would be one of only two cases in all the documentary evidence related to Ugarit and *Alašiya* where Cyprus is cast in a negative light. The other is an Akkadian tablet (RS 94.2173) from the House of Urtenu in which an *Alašiyan* messenger ostensibly was sent to secure the freedom of some Cypriots held hostage in Ugarit (Malbran-Labat 1999: 122; Lackenbacher and Malbran-Labat 2016: 41–42).

KTU 1.41 is an inscribed liver model that reads: '[liver] belonging to 'Agap-šarri when he acquired the young man from the *Alašiyan*' (Dietrich and Loretz 1969: 173–174). Here it may be noted that in Amarna Letter EA 35, the king of *Alašiya* asks the pharaoh to send him 'one of the experts in vulture augury' (Moran in Knapp 1996b: 22). Finally, a Hurrian-language text written in the Ugaritic script (RS 24.274) lists sacred objects and offerings made to the west Semitic deity El and to *atnd eni Alashiyahhe*, 'the father, god of *Alašiya*', followed by the god of Amurru and the god of Ugarit (Laroche 1968: 504–507; Kilmer and Stefanini in Knapp 1996b: 41).

POLITICS

The documents discussed in this section — all in Akkadian — treat not just political matters but also commercial exchanges between royals as well as their personal relations, people exiled to Cyprus, and notably the hostilities that likely contributed to the downfall of the Ugaritic kingdom at the end of the LBA.

Although the political organisation of LBA Cyprus has always been debated (compare, e.g., Peltenburg 2012 and Knapp 2013: 438–447), a compromise position might view the 'king' of *Alašiya* either as a paramount leader, or else one who served as a *primus inter pares* among several regional polities of the 14th-13th centuries BC. Such a ruler might also have shared power with the *rābiṣu* ('senior prefect') (Meyer 2024). Three such officials were all in direct contact with the king of Ugarit: Ešuwara (RS 20.18), Šinaš (RS 94.2173) and Šangiwa (RS 94.2447+), the last a letter sent to Niqmaddu III (Singer 1999: 691–693; Yon 2007: 18–19, n.12). It may also be noted that Amarna Letter EA 40 was sent by an unnamed *rābiṣu* of *Alašiya* to his counterpart in Egypt.

The letter (RS 94.2475) that Kušmešuša, king of *Alašiya*, sent to Niqmaddu III of Ugarit in the late 13th century BC involves commercial exchange between the two polities. Amongst other matters, the letter states that 33 ingots of copper were sent to Niqmaddu as *šulmanu*, a royal 'greeting gift' (copper is also listed as *šulmanu* in Amarna Letters EA 35, 37 and 40). These ingots are recorded as weighing 30 talents and 6500 shekels. Based on weight standards for Ugarit and Alalakh (50 shekels per mina, 60 minas per talent, thus 3000 shekels in one talent—Alberti and Parise 2005: 389), the ingots in question would have weighed just under one talent each (Singer 2006: 255). Along with a host of other data, material as well as documentary, this letter offers an impression of how Cyprus's richly endowed coastal towns — gateway centres like Enkomi, Hala Sultan Tekke, Kition and Maroni — were able to capitalise on an expanded eastern Mediterranean interaction sphere, involving at a minimum the Levant, Egypt and the Aegean (see Figure 10, below).

That *Alašiya* served as a place of exile for high-ranking members of Ugaritic society is clear from three separate documents found at Ugarit. Two Akkadian diplomatic texts (RS 17.35; RS 17.352) indicate that Ahat-Milku, the queen of Ugarit, exiled two of her sons to *Alašiya* because they had committed an offense against the queen and their (presumably younger) brother, king Ammištamru II (ruled ca. 1260-1235 BC) (Beckman 1996: no. 35; Singer 1999: 678–680). The brothers were compelled to swear their agreement before 'Ishtar of the steppe', a

Semitic (or specifically Ugaritian?) deity (Liverani 1962: 103–104). RS 17.352 was ratified by Ini-Tešub, Ammištamru's contemporary at Carchemish. RS 17.35 was ratified by Tudḫaliya IV, the same Hittite king who implemented a treaty with *Alašiya* (Hittite text KBo XII 39 — see Güterbock 1967). The exiled brothers received their share of a rich inheritance, but the nature of their offence (perhaps a struggle for the throne of Ugarit) is never mentioned (Singer 1999: 680). Nonetheless, RS 17.352 stipulates that the exiled brothers and their heirs could never lay claim to Ammištamru's or his heirs' share of the inheritance, which most likely included the throne of Ugarit.

Five further Akkadian texts related to *Alašiya* are concerned with a series of land battles and seaborne attacks on Ugarit towards the end of the 13th century BC, and with relations between Ugarit and Cyprus at that time. The texts in question are RSL 1, RS 20.238, RS 20.18, RS 34.129 and RS 94.2169, the last one from the House of Urtenu (Cifola 1994: 11; Beckman, in Knapp 1996b: 27; Cohen 2021: 57–58; Roche-Hawley 2023: 46–47). RSL 1 contains a warning sent by an unnamed king to Ammurapi, last king of Ugarit (ca. 1215-1190 BC), indicating that enemy ships had been sighted at sea and that, consequently, he ought to fortify his towns and garrison them with infantry and chariotry. Singer (1999: 721–722; see also Cohen 2021: 52–53) suggested that this enemy must refer to the so-called 'sea peoples', particularly to the *Šikila*, defined in Akkadian text RS 34.129 as people 'who live on ships' (Dietrich and Loretz 1978). Petrographic analyses have indicated that the clay of RSL 1 may have stemmed from dolerite-derived deposits within the Troodos mountains (Goren et al. 2004: 55–57); if accurate, this warning emanated from Cyprus.

RS 20.238 seems to be the reply to RSL 1 (Beckman in Knapp 1996b: 27). Here the king of Ugarit informed the king of *Alašiya* that seven enemy ships had already set fire to towns and devastated the countryside around Ugarit. The Ugaritic king also asked his counterpart to inform him if any further ships had been spotted around Cyprus. In this document, the king of Ugarit addressed the king of *Alašiya* as his 'father', just as Niqmaddu III, king of Ugarit, did in a letter (RS 20.168) addressed to the king of *Alašiya*. At the very least, this nomenclature would seem to acknowledge some level of hierarchy between the two royal courts (Liverani 1983; Singer 1999: 720; Meyer 2024). Sürenhagen (2001: 255–256), however, argued persuasively that these terms may reflect some sort of kinship relations. The final text, RS 94.2169, echoes the information relayed in RS 20.238: the king of Ugarit writes to an unknown king (or perhaps to the Hittite viceroy at Carchemish?) stating that the enemy forces are now stationed at *Ra'šu* (Ras ibn Hani?) whilst an advance force has gone to Ugarit itself (Cohen 2021: 58; Roche-Hawley 2023: 47). All three texts — RSL 1, RS 20.238, RS 94.2169 — indicate that the king of *Alašiya* was well informed of ship and troop movements involving Ugarit and knew that an 'enemy' was moving eastward by sea toward the Levantine coast, ultimately establishing itself at the gates of Ugarit.

Finally, the *rābiṣu* of *Alašiya*, Ešuwara, sent another letter (RS 20.18 — Beckman in Knapp 1996a: 27) to the king of Ugarit, mentioning 'this thing' or 'transgression' that the enemy had carried out against the people and ships of Cyprus. Ešuwara added that he was not to blame for any troubles that might affect

Ugarit, but warned that 20 more ships, which had approached 'the mountain', failed to make a stand and had suddenly set off again, so the king of Ugarit should be aware of potential trouble ahead. Roche-Hawley (2023: 47) curiously translates this passage as 20 boats 'hiding in the mountains', whereas Yamasaki (2023: 109) sensibly suggests that 'the mountain' may represent a reference point to the island's Troodos Mountains, in particular Mount Olympus, its highest peak.

PROFESSIONS

This section deals with a range of goods exchanged between Ugarit and Cyprus, with sales or transfers of land, and with messengers and scribes. The merchants of Ugarit are treated separately, in the discussion section that follows (Chapter 7: *The Merchants of Ugarit and Cyprus*).

A series of Ugaritic and Akkadian cuneiform texts record various goods exchanged between *Alašiya* and Ugarit. From Ugarit to *Alašiya*, the various exchanges involved horses (RS 34.153, but see further below), ships (RS 18.113A), two pitchers and a pot containing unknown provisions (RS 15.39, RS 15.96, see further below), and 660 measures of oil for 'Abrm the *Alashiyan*' (RS 18.42, a bill of lading listing the cargo of a ship; Sauvage 2006: 621 suggests only 160 jars). From *Alašiya* to Ugarit, the goods transferred include several unknown items and three trowels (RS 18.119). RS 20.168 indicates that oil and *tannu*-vessels were exchanged between *Alašiya* and Ugarit, but the text is not clear in which direction. Yon (2000: 192) added that oil and wheat were sent from *Alašiya* to Ugarit.

Sauvage (2012: 130) noted that a commerce in (olive) oil between Cyprus and Ugarit is well attested. In Ugaritic text RS 18.42, the exchange may not be concerned with commerce but rather with palatial collection and redistribution of (olive) oil in the form of rations. In Akkadian text RS 20.168, the oil was delivered by an emissary. Sauvage (2012: 131 n. 918) also notes that 'food' (*'akl*) was sent from Ugarit to (most likely) Cyprus, citing Ugaritic text RS 18.147. This text, particularly difficult to interpret (see, e.g., Virolleaud 1965: 87–88; Schaeffer 1968: 722–725) was written by one *Pgn* to the king of Ugarit; Yon (2013: 209 n. 16, 213 table 1) suggested that *Pgn* might be the name of a king of Cyprus (see also Ferrara 2015: 113). Be that as it may, another text (RS 94.2392+94.2400), also in Ugaritic, reportedly concerns the sale of ebony wood, which was to be exchanged for 51 *kaddu* 'measures' (more likely 'jars') of oil (Bordreuil and Pardee 2009: 276–277; Sauvage 2012: 149; cf. Monroe 2016 on Ugaritic *kadu* as 'jar'). The last section of this text concerns an exchange where the unit of measure of oil for the *Alašiyan* is not specified, perhaps because the amount was known to all involved.

An Akkadian text from Ugarit (RS 34.153 — Beckman in Knapp 1996b: 28) mentions (1) an exchange of horses involving the king of Ugarit and a messenger from *Alašiya*, and (2) the transhipment of *Alašiyan* copper to Emar, a major LBA centre situated on the banks of the Upper Euphrates River, at the juncture of land-based trading routes. Monroe (2009: 188–189) interpreted this letter from Urtenu's archive to mean that the author of the letter accompanied a shipment of horses from *Alašiya* to the king of Ugarit, but the text could also be interpreted to mean that the horses were sent to *Alašiya* (Yon 2003: 48).

Ugaritic text (RS 18.113A) is a fragmentary royal letter to the king (of Ugarit?), invoking 'the gods of *Alašiya*' (Ba'al, Šapaš, Athtart, Anat) and dealing with the sale of ships, presumably by Ugarit's harbour-master to a merchant from *Alašiya*; this transaction required the approval of the king of Ugarit (Knapp 1983; Singer 1999: 678; Monroe 2009: 115). Pardee (2023: 72) points out that the identity of the merchant is not preserved in the long, preceding fragmentary passage, and thus it is unclear whether he was competing with the Ugaritic king's envoy (and thus an *Alašiyan*, not a Ugaritian) or rather was part of a local entourage seeking to acquire boats. RS 18.119 is an inventory list (in Ugaritic) listing the contents of a ship from *Alašiya* moored in the port of 'Atlg. Lines 3 and 4 list '15 talents of…' and '3 talents of …', but the commodity is broken. Given that 'talent' is frequently used to indicate quantities of metal, perhaps this commodity was copper (see also Singer 1999: 676). An Ugaritic tablet (RS 18.24) found in the royal palace that mentions Urtenu is concerned with a delivery of copper and tin to *Bi'ruti* (perhaps to be equated with Ras ibn Hani, not Beirut — Bounni et al. 1998: 96).

Two Akkadian legal documents from Ugarit (RS 17.36, RS 17.149) treat the sale or transfer of land and property (Nougayrol et al. 1968: 9–11). These documents do not mention *Alašiya* but bear impressions from Cypriot style cylinder seals that seem to have been used before the tablets were inscribed: the cuneiform signs on RS 17.149 have obscured the lower part of the seal design (Smith 1994: 178). Smith (1994: 181, n. 157) observed that the scene on this seal ('mistress of animals' motif) has stylistic parallels on other Cypriot cylinder seals common both in Ugarit and on Cyprus, and thus suggested these impressions may signal the presence of Cypriot merchants or administrators at Ugarit during 14th-13th centuries BC. In any case, these seal impressions are atypical, as most official, sealed documents from Ugarit were impressed with the local ruler's dynastic seal.

The 1994 Ras Shamra excavations recovered at least six Akkadian tablets sent to Ugarit by the king of *Alašiya* or two of his viziers. From these, it seems clear that some people from Cyprus were established in Ugarit for commercial purposes. Two of these tablets refer to the circulation of messengers between Ugarit and *Alašiya*. One was a letter of accreditation, evidently for an *Alašiyan* messenger who was to secure the freedom of Cypriots held in Ugarit (RS 94.2173). The other (RS 94.2447++), addressed to Niqmaddu III, mentions the dispatch of a royal messenger to *Alašiya* concerning a shipment of horses (Malbran-Labat 1999: 122). The last may be compared to RS 34.153, in which the king of Ugarit delivered horses to an *Alašiyan* messenger for dispatch to Cyprus (see above). RS 94.2177+2491 mentions a scribe from Ugarit stationed in the royal court at *Alašiya*: he asked for five new chairs and a fine table to be sent to him from Ugarit, perhaps because the town's craftspeople included specialised cabinet makers (Bordreuil and Malbran-Labat 1995: 445). Finally, RS 94.2561 is a letter addressed to 'my brother' 'Uzzīnu, a well-known *sākinu* at Ugarit, from his *Alašiyan* counterpart, Kinniki. 'Uzzīnu is asked to handle a matter regarding textiles acquired by Cypriots two years previously, and to cease taxing Cypriot merchants upon their arrival in Ugarit (Lackenbacher and Malbran-Labat 2016: 152–154; Pardee 2023: 80).

CHAPTER 7

MATERIAL AND MERCANTILE CONNECTIVITY IN THE LATE BRONZE AGE EASTERN MEDITERRANEAN

Is the Old Assyrian mercantile system a unique case, or is the entrepreneurial nature of trade, in which the state is an interested but not organizing agent, a feature of other periods of ... history? (Yoffee 2014: 216)

... the larger picture of Late Bronze Age trade reveals rulers and merchants, together with their families, partners and various customers, connected in material and immaterial webs. (Monroe 2015: 45, emphasis added)

Monroe (2015: 46) goes on to say that maritime traders entangled everyone, and that their ships carried goods, wealth and information across the waves to their trading partners, mercantile firms, households and consumers. How does this view of LBA maritime trade, based largely on textual evidence from Ugarit, square with the material (and immaterial) evidence compiled in the present study? How and to what extent did the Cypriot polity, its rulers, communities, households and merchants, differ from the configuration at Ugarit? What sort of capital accumulation and technological know-how were necessary to build the ships and maintain the merchants and fleets in the existing webs of exchange? How would the 'great kings' (e.g., of Egypt, Hittite Anatolia, Assyria) who operated in Levantine coastal polities such as Ugarit have reacted when Cypriot copper began to supply an eastern Mediterranean network of exchange around 1500 BC (Monroe 2015: 36; see also Sherratt and Sherratt 1991: 368–373)? How pervasive and influential were elite merchants (such as Ugarit's Rap'anu, Rašap-abu, Urtenu and Yabninu) in what Monroe (2015: 40–41) termed the 'entrepreneurial sphere' that encompassed several groups of people with similar relations and access to the means of production and exchange?

Much of the 'story' (or stories) of relations between Cyprus and Ugarit that exists in the literature has been driven by the textual evidence from Ugarit. This results partly from the haphazard way in which Ugarit's material record was published (or not), a situation echoed to some extent by the early excavations at Enkomi on Cyprus. To gain a clearer picture of the differences in — and relations between — the Cypriot and Ugaritic polities, I begin by looking more closely at the textual and material evidence from Ugarit, and then consider the material record of Cyprus, insofar as it pertains to merchants.

THE MERCHANTS OF UGARIT AND CYPRUS

Documentary evidence regarding the merchants that dwelt in or operated out of Ugarit and its ports (Minet el-Beidha–*Ma'ḥadu*, Ras Ibn Hani) is extensive (e.g., Astour 1972; Schloen 2001; Monroe 2009, 2015; Bell 2012), and continues to be a focal point of interest. Pardee's (2023) recent study on the merchants of Ugarit, for example, is exhaustive and reflects decades of work on both the 'logo-syllabic' (Akkadian) and alphabetic (Ugaritic) texts. From his unique, primarily philological perspective, Pardee examines the role of both local and international merchants in the movement of merchandise into, through and beyond the kingdom of Ugarit. His focus is on the term(s) for merchant, mainly the *mkrm* (Sumerian DAM.GÀR, Akkadian *tamkāru*), the "primary cogs in the commercial machinery by which merchandise moved in and through the kingdom" (Pardee 2023: 42). In his view, the texts from Ras Shamra refer primarily to cases of 'professional' merchants in regular service to the royal administration (a more accurate term might be 'commercial agents'), secondarily to individuals who operated independently and whose profits might be subject to taxation at royal discretion (Pardee 2023: 90, 92, 94–95). In his words: "they [*mkrm*] thus were clearly one of the occupational categories reflecting the economic interests of the royal administration and the structural components of what might be called the upper echelons of the workforce of the kingdom" (Pardee 2023: 89).

Regarding relations with Cyprus specifically, Singer (1999: 677) suggested that Ugarit's maritime trade with the island was managed by wealthy merchants like Urtenu or Yabninu. In Yabninu's house, two Cypro-Minoan, five Ugaritic and over 60 Akkadian documents were uncovered, many of which were economic records related to overseas trade. Urtenu's house contained a range of Cypriot wares, several documents recording exchange activities with Cyprus and two 'labels' written in Cypro-Minoan. Like Yabninu, Urtenu seems to have been involved in importing or exporting Cypriot goods and raw materials. The 200 tablets from the House of Rap'anu included much of the international correspondence from Cyprus. From the surface above the House of Rašap-Abu came a small clay tablet bearing a Cypro-Minoan inscription (RS 17.06): as harbour-master, Rašap-Abu would have dealt with many of the ships and merchants, Cypriot or otherwise, entering or leaving the harbour(s) at Ugarit. These elite merchants indubitably formed part of Monroe's entrepreneurial sphere.

Based on the ceramic evidence from two possible storage areas at Minet el-Beidha — (1) deposit 213 with its abundant Base-ring wares; (2) *entrepôt aux 80 jarres* (i.e., Levantine CJs — see Figure 4, above), Sauvage (2006: 22) first posited that they might be seen as the warehouses of local merchants and foreign traders. The foreign group would have stocked their goods in such rooms before sending them home or selling them in Ugarit. In a reassessment of the *entrepôt aux 80 jarres*, Sauvage (2015: 73) suggested this deposit may correspond to an area where deliveries of oil or wine, produced in a nearby workshop, were prepared for distribution. Storing jars in this manner seems to correspond with some administrative texts which, according to Pardee (2012: 184), indicate that the port at Minet el-Beidha was under royal jurisdiction. The area around this deposit thus might be regarded as a workshop for producing oil and wine, where certain pieces were temporarily stored to expedite delivery — local or international — of this specific merchandise. Whatever the case may have been concerning the finds in these two deposits, we may still imagine — along with Sauvage (2006) — that imported goods were stored separately from local products. In turn, we may speculate whether private merchants specialised in specific kinds of goods. Thus, we might conclude that elite merchants involved in the exchange of prestigious goods on an international scale should be distinguished from those who dealt with other products on a strictly local basis.

The exchange system through which Cypriot copper arrived in Ugarit may have involved either *Alašiyan* or Ugaritic merchants, or both. Sauvage (2012: 152) suggested that the bulk of copper consumed throughout the Levant likely originated on Cyprus but was transhipped through Ugarit. The cuneiform archives from Ugarit indeed attest to a trade in copper and tin (e.g., RS 94.2475), not only for local consumption but also for the onward movement of these metals (e.g., RS 34.153). Based on her PhD research, Bell (2006: 85–87) argued that Ugarit (along with Ras Ibn Hani) was the only Levantine coastal site that could be identified as a major recipient of both copper and tin consignments. In the most general terms and leaving aside other key factors and caveats, the value of Cypriot copper seems to have been highest in Egypt but in Ugarit had only about a half or, at different times, even a quarter of that value (Courtois et al. 1986: 65; Papasavvas 2018; 2021: 133 table 1, 136); in other words, Ugarit was an ideal place to buy Cypriot copper (if not all manner of other materials and goods). Prices, moreover, may have varied, if we may extrapolate from the quality of copper — e.g., the 'mountain', 'refined' or 'pure' copper of *Alašiya* — mentioned in earlier Akkadian documents from Mari and Babylonia (Sasson, in Knapp 1996b: 17–19).

Merchants — be they Cypriot, Ugaritic, or otherwise — would have been aware of the current values and equivalencies of all metals, including copper, exchanged within the networks where they conducted their business. Some Levantine merchants (Akkadian *tamkāru*), not least those of Ugarit, lived aboard ships or travelled in caravans (Monroe 2015: 11–15), whilst others dwelt in the harbour towns where they plied their trade. The harbour community (Akkadian *kāru*) would have accommodated a variety of maritime merchants and traders who, as Monroe (2009: 280; 2011: 87–88) argued, operated in a 'liminal' space between the sea and the shore.

Some cuneiform records from Ugarit (e.g., RS 18.113A) reveal that independent merchants or their assistants (*mkrm, bdlm, mzrġlm*) invested in ships and cargoes like the one that sank at Uluburun (Astour 1972; Monroe 2015: 25; Pardee 2012; 2023: 74, 82). Commercial agents like these also invested in ventures on behalf of the Ugaritic king whilst others (*tamkāru ša mandatti*) may have collected tribute for the state (Monroe 2009: 181–189; 2011: 91–95); Pardee (2023: 74–75, and n.123) argues strenuously that *ša mandatti* should be understood to refer to "merchants operating as commercial agents for their king, their expedition funded by him."

When shipments of goods, imported or exported, involved the crown at Ugarit (e.g., RS 18.119, RS 18.113A), royal as well as merchant capital might be invested; above all, however, such exchanges required merchant expertise. The role of the state in maritime trade at Ugarit thus seems to have been indirect, or 'symbiotic', and was typically overseen by a *sākinu* ('prefect') (van Soldt 2002; Monroe 2011: 94; 2015: 25). Although the crown sought to invest in and tax merchants and commerce to varying degrees (one exception being Sinaranu and his ship with goods coming from Crete — RS 16.238+254), it does not seem to have kept a fleet of vessels specifically designated for trading ventures. Such fleets, if they existed, must have belonged to the merchants themselves. Although no documents indicate who had the expertise to build and maintain these ships, RS 18.113A indicates that the harbour-master of Ugarit sold ships, in this case to a merchant from *Alašiya* (but cf. Pardee 2012; 2023: 72).

Whilst most Ugaritic merchants did not belong to a single socioeconomic group, some seem to have attained elite status whilst others held state or civic offices. The wealthiest were those who carried out state business and were paid in silver — the 'merchants of the king' (*tamkāru ša šarri* — Monroe 2009: 282). Perhaps Urtenu, Yabninu, Rap'anu and Rašap-Abu were amongst them — all elite merchants who played multiple roles within the political economy, at times serving under palatial contract, at other times operating on an entrepreneurial basis. McGeough (2015: 93–94) discussed various commercial, royal and diplomatic activities and transactions that involved Yabninu and Urtenu (see also Matoïan 2021c: 140–141, 144).

Urtenu might be seen as the preeminent prefect, an oligarch with economic ties to various people or polities throughout the Levant, Cyprus, Egypt and Anatolia. Roche-Hawley (2023: 44–45) emphasizes that texts from the House of Urtenu dealing with maritime commerce and navigation far exceed those found in any other context at Ugarit: 40 in number, including six concerned specifically with Cyprus. In Pardee's (2023:90) view, the best example of commercial activity at Ugarit — whether conducted by Ugaritic or foreign merchants — is represented by "… the 'firm' run primarily, as far as can be determined by examination of known texts, from the House of 'Urtēnu." Indeed, from the perspective of all the foreign merchants who had to deal with Urtenu, "he was effectively 'the state'" (Monroe 2015: 34). As already emphasized, most of these elite merchants dwelt in elaborate houses where they stored goods to be exchanged, kept documentary archives of their diverse transactions (and seals to identify themselves or their goods), and engaged their families in various aspects of their business (Monroe 2009: 240, 283; Bell 2012: 182–184). The geographic orbit in which these merchants operated extended from the Aegean, Cyprus and inner Anatolia in the west, to upper Mesopotamia in the east, and to Egypt in the south (Bell 2012: 184 and table 19.1); all manner of international goods came into or through Ugarit via this orbit (McGeough 2015: 91).

All this documentary evidence reveals the diversity of Ugarit's social, economic and political links with Cyprus during the 14th-13th centuries BC. These same documents also demonstrate that people of Cypriot origin (or named after the island) were engaged in multiple mercantile, administrative and diplomatic matters at Ugarit.

Turning to the merchants and mercantile communities of Cyprus, Knapp and Meyer (2023) argued that, already during the LC I period (ca. 1600-1500/1450 BC), Cypriot as well as Levantine merchants were engaged in burgeoning international trade networks. Between ca. 1500-1350 BC, Cyprus's export economy was transformed, and new forms of economic power developed as a result of increased intra-island and external trade. Amongst the material markers of Cyprus's new, more sophisticated export economy, shipping logistics and the consumer needs involved, we might single out: (1) the prominence of technologically improved White Slip II hemispheric bowls in Levantine ports (including at least 216 at Ugarit and Minet el-Beidha — see Table 1, above) (Artzy 2001b; Yon 2001; Renson et al. 2013), and (2) the increased numbers of locally produced, 'artistically competent', bronze, ivory and faience artefacts, most commonly found in mortuary deposits (Peltenburg 2007; Caubet 2009; Papasavvas 2012).

In the latter part of the 13th century BC, this trend towards diversified industrialised production in support of mercantile activities is attested by (1) the scale of textile manufacture at Hala Sultan Tekke (Sabatini, in Fischer and Bürge 2018: 431–455) and (2) the emergence of another new industry in bronze tripods and stands (Papasavvas 2003). As Cyprus reached the acme of metallurgical production towards the end of the 13th century BC — evident in the prevalence of bronze objects designed for export as well as for internal consumption (Papasavvas 2012: 120–121; Charalambous et al. 2014; Ioannides et al. 2024), private merchants may already have come into their own (Meneghetti 2022-23: 105). In other words, by the end of the LBA, the producers and merchants of Cyprus were engaged in a mercantile network involving not only raw materials (e.g., copper, timber, perhaps purple dye), but also and increasingly goods that were manufactured locally (e.g., pottery wares, bronze objects, ivory products, textiles). This calls to mind what Sherratt and Sherratt (1991: 358–359) defined as a trading network with a 'full linkage' productive base.

Mercantile as well as political relations between Cyprus and Ugarit after ca. 1400 BC are evident in several Akkadian and Ugaritic texts from Ugarit (full presentation above); for example, Cypriot ships sent cargoes of copper, grain, oil and perhaps wine to Ugarit (Knapp 1983: 42–43), whilst Kušmešuša, king of Cyprus, sent 33 copper ingots to Niqmaddu, king of Ugarit (Lackenbacher and Malbran-Labat 2016: 38–41). The ports of Cyprus not only offered Bronze Age merchants — Cypriot, Ugaritic, or otherwise — access to the island's copper ores, but also provided them with meeting points where they could monitor fluctuations in supply and demand. The market potential of networked Cypriot ports like Enkomi, Kition, Maroni and Hala Sultan Tekke meant that merchants could procure a wide range of manufactured goods and raw materials — domestic and foreign — that ensured economically viable ventures. Knapp and Meyer (2023: 320–324) also identified multiple structures in these ports that could have accommodated local merchants and at the same time provided the capacity for foreign merchants to shelter, store their goods and conduct their business, e.g., at Kalavasos *Ayios Dhimitrios* (Building III), Maroni *Tsaroukkas* (Building 1), Maa *Palaeokastro* (Buildings II, III) (Figure 9), Hala Sultan Tekke *Vyzakia* (CQ 1, Building C) and Kition ('Temple' 1).

I turn now to consider other aspects of the evidence presented in this study, particularly as it relates to maritime spheres of interaction and the agents and actors operating in the mercantile worlds of the LBA eastern Mediterranean.

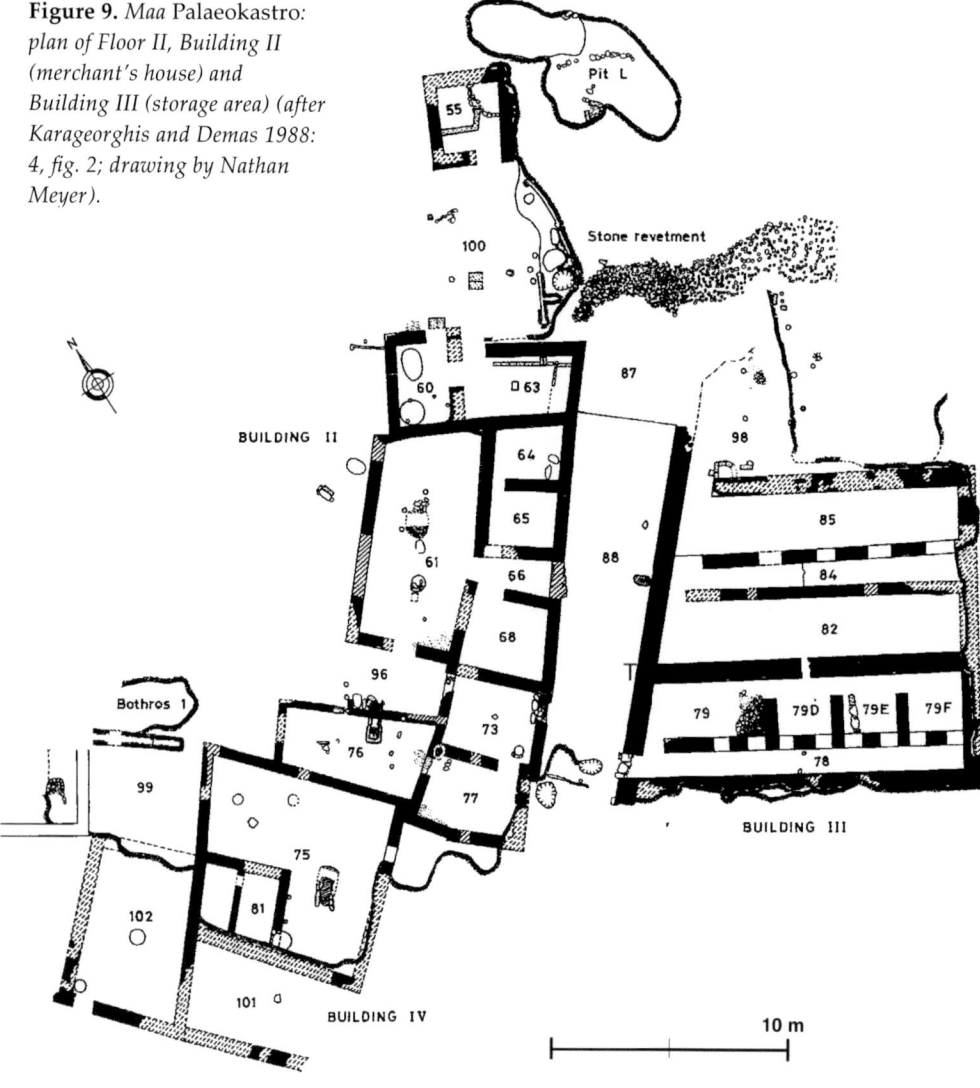

Figure 9. *Maa* Palaeokastro: plan of Floor II, Building II (merchant's house) and Building III (storage area) (after Karageorghis and Demas 1988: 4, fig. 2; drawing by Nathan Meyer).

MARITIME SPHERE(S) OF INTERACTION

Based on the amounts of LBA Aegean painted pottery found at sites throughout the Aegean and eastern Mediterranean, Broodbank (2013: 413) estimated that 40-50 urban trading centres operated in the area stretching from the Nile Delta through the Levant, southern coastal Anatolia and Cyprus to the Aegean. Countless further, mainly coastal communities — smaller ports, anchorages or havens (Demesticha 2022) — comprised the wider maritime spheres of interaction that typified the mercantile world of the LBA eastern Mediterranean. The expansion of maritime trade during this era and the accumulation of wealth that followed in its wake must have coincided with or indeed underlaid other social changes, not least a sharp rise in entrepreneurial activity.

Three recent studies have outlined some possible overlapping and interlocking regional spheres of interaction in the Bronze Age eastern Mediterranean (Knapp and Demesticha 2017: 31–32, 151–153; Knapp 2022; Knapp et al. 2022). Based on the information presented in the present study, we may refine those simplified spheres to one focused mainly on Cyprus and Ugarit, and another embracing Cyprus, the coasts of southern Anatolia and the Levant, extending perhaps to the Egyptian delta (Figure 10).

Such abstract schemes, however, tell us little about the mechanisms that drove such trade or indeed about the identity of the merchants or the home port(s) of the ships involved. In considering the range of maritime interaction spheres that existed in the LBA eastern Mediterranean, the more general question arises of differences between local, coastal-oriented ventures versus direct, long-distance sailing expeditions (Arnaud 2011: 61; see also Calvo-Trias and Galmés-Alba 2024:

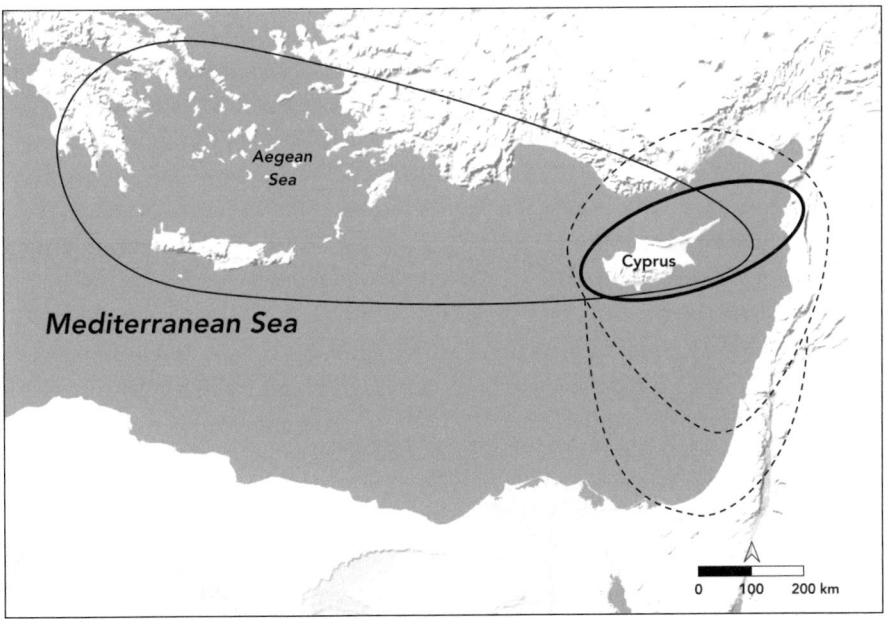

Figure 10. *Late Bronze Age Eastern Mediterranean spheres of interaction (prepared by Nathan Meyer).*

26–28). Arnaud (2005: 114, 118–121) argued that the two types of trade were often combined: regional and interregional trade necessitated larger ships, more sophisticated nautical expertise, and in the end also entailed less economic risk (Monroe 2011: 93). The breadth and complexity of these interaction spheres intensified and expanded through time, reaching their greatest extent during the 13th century BC. The trade was bidirectional if not multi-directional, and some goods — e.g., metals, ores, MTCs, organic goods — seem to have travelled east and west, north and south. Consider the most trenchant example: the finds on the Uluburun shipwreck represent nine or ten different cultures, from Cypriot oxhide ingots to Levantine anchors to a variety of raw materials and luxury goods (gold, silver, tin, cobalt, ivory, amber, ostrich eggs) from several other, different origins. In Ward's (2010: 155–156) view, although the Uluburun ship represents a prime example of directional (long-distance) trade by some of the LBA's most 'conspicuous consumers', it is still not possible to say who captained the ship, how the cargo was financed or where it was headed.

Based on her long-term study of stone anchors from Ugarit and Kition, Frost (1985, 1991: 370–371) concluded that, amongst the LBA merchant ships that plied the eastern Mediterranean, some of the largest must have been of Levantine (Ugarit, Byblos) and Cypriot origin. Knapp and Demesticha (2017: 166) argued that the sailing vessels involved in bulk maritime transport (i.e., oxhide ingots, Canaanite Jars and other MTCs—see also Sherratt and Sherratt 1991) during the LBA in the eastern Mediterranean involved at least two components: (1) small independent boats sailing short distances over opportunistic routes, and (2) large ships, heavily capitalised, with major cargoes sailing long-distance international routes. The latter class of vessel not only docked at but relied upon ports like Ugarit and Tel Abu Hawam in the Levant, and Enkomi, Kition and Hala Sultan Tekke on Cyprus.

The interaction spheres in which Ugarit and various Cypriot ports — and their merchants — were involved were complex and multi-dimensional, private as well as state-supported or influenced. Akkadian texts from Ugarit mention merchant representatives (RS 16.126B+257+258), royal merchants (RS 17.146), merchants granted tax-free status (RS 16.386), an exchange of horses involving the king of Ugarit and an *Alašiyan* messenger (RS 34.153), an exchange of textiles with *Alašiya* along with a complaint about *Alašiyan* merchants being taxed at Ugarit (RS 94.2561), and even one merchant from Ugarit (Sinaranu) whose Cretan goods were exempt from taxes (RS 16.238+254) — although there is no direct indication that Sinaranu's ship was of Levantine origin. The letter (RS 94.2475) sent by Kušmešuša, king of *Alašiya*, to Niqmaddu III, king of Ugarit, reveals the close commercial if not familial links between two of the main polities in the eastern Mediterranean interaction sphere, the core subjects of this study.

Two Akkadian legal documents (RS 17.36, RS 17.149) that bear Cypriot style cylinder seal impressions may indicate that Cypriot merchants worked out of Ugarit (Smith 1994: 181, n. 157). Ugaritic documents from Ugarit, less informative and more difficult of interpretation, mention an *Alašiyan* (?) merchant buying ships (KTU 2.42+2.43–RS 18.113A+B), a 'catalogue' of ships (in Ma'ḥadu) listing their captains (KTU 4.81–RS 11.779) and a list of merchants (*mkrm* — KTU 4.263–RS 17.49; see Pardee 2023: 63–64 for a detailed analysis). Ugaritic text KTU 4.149 may refer to wine provisions for foreign diplomats or merchants returning home to Cyprus and Anatolia (Matoïan and Vita 2018: 311–313). Since Cypro-Minoan texts remain undeciphered, there are no interpretable documents from Cyprus that refer to the Levant, only the four CM tablets (of 12 known CM inscriptions) found at Ugarit.

Regarding the nationality of the merchants and origin of the ships that carried them, it seems reasonable to propose that the maritime interaction spheres of the LBA eastern Mediterranean operated largely through initiatives undertaken by various merchants, ship-owners, emissaries or other mercantile agents from multiple coastal or island polities; major, land-based powers such as the Hittite state or New Kingdom Egypt had little beyond nominal control over them (Wachsmann 1998: 10). As we have seen, the case of Ugarit is rather different: some merchants served as commercial agents for the king whilst others — like Uretnu and Yabninu — operated (semi-)independently. Ugarit's entire political regime seems mercantile in orientation and outlook: if so, the king's relationship with local merchants would simply be a variant of his relationship with foreign merchants. The port facilities (including store houses) were hospitable places for local and international trade, and a variety of goods was available; merchants and their goods were protected; formal trade agreements existed, and taxes seem to have been bearable (Nathan Meyer, pers. comm., April 2024).

I have argued elsewhere that there were no maritime thalassocracies in the LBA eastern Mediterranean, whether Cypriot, Levantine, Egyptian or Minoan (Knapp 1993). Whilst overt attempts by major, land-based powers to control trade might be subverted through resistance, corruption or simply shifting the location of the trade emporium, historically, excessive freedom of trade is often reined in by social, political or ideological regulation (Oka and Kusimba 2008: 366–367).

MERCANTILE WORLDS: AGENTS AND ACTORS

From the evidence gathered in this study, we might imagine that a Bronze Age ship built in Ugarit was owned by a Cypriot (RS 18.113A+B), captained by a Canaanite (RS 16.238+254) or perhaps by the *Šikila* 'who live on ships' (RS 34.129). Our hypothetical ship could have carried wine, olive oil and grain (RS 15.39, RS 20.168, RS 20.212, RS 26.158), horses (RS 34.153), if not metals (RS 18.24, RS 94.2475) and pottery containers (RS 18.42, RS 94.2392+ 94.2400), and was en route to *Bi'ruti* (Beirut? or Ras Ibn Hani, and thus back to Ugarit?) (RS 18.24, RS 16.238+254) or to Cilicia (RS 20.212, RS 26.158).

Accepting that some of the largest mercantile vessels operating in the eastern Mediterranean were of Levantine or Cypriot origin (Frost 1991: 370–371), Votruba (2019: 233) noted (see above) that 75% of the PSF3SA-type stone anchors datable to the 2nd millennium BC were either found on Cyprus or have been attributed to it. All other examples of this type of anchor derive from the tell at Ugarit or from Minet el-Beidha. Although Votruba (2019: 234) suggested that Levantine sailors might have made and dedicated the PSAs found at Kition, the specific identities of the merchants, sailors or captains of the ships bearing these anchors may never be known securely. Nonetheless, multiple streams of material and documentary evidence indicate that merchants and mariners from Cyprus and Ugarit repeatedly plied the sea lanes of the eastern Mediterranean during the LBA.

How might we envision the trade mechanisms operating in a LBA mercantile system? Panagiotopoulos (2011: 40–41) distinguished two such mechanisms: (1) closed networks that included gift exchanges amongst the major states of the LBA (Egypt, Hittite Anatolia, Mitanni, Assyria, Babylonia) and (2) open networks of long-distance trade between and amongst these major polities and other, smaller states (e.g., Cyprus, Levantine coastal sites). The former are seen to be diplomatic and sociopolitical in nature, the latter largely economic or mercantile in nature. Although the open networks might also have involved reciprocity, they were more flexible than the closed networks and operated through multiple modes of exchange with more trading partners that included diverse types of polities. Panagiotopoulos maintained that the smaller-scale polities of the Levant and the Aegean (and presumably Cyprus, which he doesn't mention) contributed more to the cosmopolitanism of this era than did any of the major powers. On the one hand, Panagiotopoulos's views on open and closed networks make it possible to consider the links between LBA Cyprus and Ugarit as part of an open system and a broader mercantile world. On the other hand, given the wide array of raw materials, finished products and other organic and inorganic products listed in the cuneiform documentary evidence of the 'great kings' (Liverani 1990), his views might be challenged.

Some of the key players — merchants paramount amongst them — involved in the diverse systems of exchange in the Mediterranean seem to have invested in developing and branding certain of their local products, to attract or fulfil demand within the wider system(s) (on branding practices generally, Bevan and Wengrow 2010; on Cyprus specifically, Meneghetti 2022-23). Amongst such products from Cyprus or the Levant are the following:

- the blistered surface of copper oxhide ingots, and CM (or other) marks on them
- Cypriot Base-ring juglets (opium?)
- Cretan octopus motif on Transport Stirrup Jars (TSJs) found on Cyprus and in Levant
- medium-sized, Argolid-produced TSJs with CM signs (for the Cypriot market?)
- *kupirijo* goods listed on Linear B tablets (honey, unguents, vases destined for Cyprus?)
- small Mycenaean stirrup jars (for scented oils)
- Mycenaean amphoroid kraters with pictorial scenes (designed specifically for Cypriot and Levantine consumers?)
- potmarks (a neutral term) and potter's marks incised or painted on pottery vessels (the last two examples suggested by Meneghetti 2022-23: 107–110).

Merchants could have applied post-firing marks to identify their brands and to attract prospective buyers, thus creating a bond between maker, merchant and final consumer (Meneghetti (2022-23: 111). Alternatively, when pots were used as containers for other commodities (e.g., the Cypriot *pithoi* on the Uluburun shipwreck), any post-fired markings on them could have signalled the contents, not the containers themselves.

As Meneghetti (2022-23: 99, 101) points out, the main purpose of branding goods is to convey information about their origin, and branding practices such as the use of seals, labels and marks on pots or ingots were surely familiar to merchants and consumers within the mercantile networks of the LBA (see also Bevan 2010). Several questions remain: who were the actors involved in these practices — i.e., the producers, merchants, distributors, consumers? Might we envision what Meneghetti (2022-23: 105–106) described as a 'brand community', i.e., beyond single consumers (Muniz and O'Guinn 2001: 412), unbound by polity or geography and based on social or economic relationships amongst those who distributed or sought specific, uniquely decorated or labelled commodities?

Ferrara (2015: 113–114; 2016: 230) suggested that the Cypriot *boules* with CM marks might have been used as a type of 'identity card', perhaps bearing the names of (elite?) individuals somehow engaged in workshops or other institutions at Cypriot sites such as Enkomi, Kition, Kalavasos *Ayios Dhimitrios* and Hala Sultan Tekke. She also proposed that the name on one of the balls from Ugarit (*Pgn*) may refer to a king of *Alašiya* (likewise, Yon 2013: 209 n. 16). The fragmentary royal letter RS 18.113A indicates that some Cypriots participated in ceremonial activities at Ugarit. Other Cypriots (*alṭy* or *aldy* in Ugaritic) received food and clothing rations and so presumably resided in Ugarit, having been integrated into community life (Knapp 1983; Vita 1999: 459). CM tablet RS 20.25 (O. Masson 1969), found in the House of Rap'ānu, and possibly CM tablet RS 17.06 (O. Masson 1956) from the House of Rašap-Abu, appear to be census rolls, listing the names of Cypriot individuals to mark their origin, identity or occupation within the Ugaritic state (Ferrara 2012: 137–141). The five Akkadian tablets recovered from the House or Urtenu — sent to Ugarit by the king of *Alašiya* and two of his viziers — demonstrate the commercial roles of the messengers who circulated between these two polities.

Turning to copper oxhide ingots, we might consider an alternative view of the oxhide ingot mould uncovered at Ugarit's port of Ras ibn Hani (Bounni et al. 1998: 43–48). It seems somewhat incongruous that copper matte would have been shipped to Ugarit to produce oxhide ingots there. Could this have been a mercantile (or recycling?) operation to create and distribute the well-known brand of Cypriot copper? If so, then we either have a case of some dubious commercial practices by a merchant or manufacturer from Ugarit, or we are dealing with a mercantile 'family' that included Cypriots who felt entitled to the brand (Nathan Meyer, pers. comm., April 2024). Such a situation is perhaps hinted at in letter RS 94.2561, addressed by the Cypriot *sākinu*, Kinniki, to his counterpart and 'brother', Uzzīnu, in Ugarit.

In any case, once the (branded) oxhide ingots of Cypriot copper began to enter the wider eastern Mediterranean mercantile system, the 'great kings' who had extended their politico-economic reach into liminal zones such as the Levantine coast had to rethink their own world system (Monroe 2015: 36). Traders operating out of Ugarit made considerable payments of silver for land, concessions and exemptions based on what Monroe (2015: 37–38) termed a system of 'production for exchange'. In such a system, merchants, estates, mercantile firms, and others associated with them (landowners, artisans, shippers, boat builders) constituted an entrepreneurial sphere "...whose mode of accumulation depended on the activity of households involved in buying goods and services" (Monroe 2015: 38). Elite merchants such as Yabninu or Urtenu would have belonged to the 'upper class' (Astour 1972) of this entrepreneurial sphere, which included others who had similar relations and access to the means of production and exchange (Monroe 2015: 40–41).

The presumably Cypriot residents living in an area of Ugarit called 'Cyprus-town' (Ugaritic text RS 11.857) are also of relevance here (Monroe 2015: 31–32). The practice of adoption at Ugarit may represent one strategy to consolidate familial wealth and to establish more intimate relationships amongst households within the entrepreneurial sphere (Monroe 2015: 31); in this regard, Pardee (2023: 93–94) notes a range of textual evidence concerning the hereditary aspects of Ugarit's 'professional' group of merchants (*mkrm*). We might even envision a scenario — already suggested above — in which, by the 13th century BC, the kings of Ugarit and *Alašiya* belonged to the same commercial 'family': Levantine merchants would have been instrumental in opening up Cyprus but in time some Cypriot merchants would have become the major players as a result of wealth accumulated from the metals trade, engaging Ugarit as a primary locus to secure their distribution network (Nathan Meyer, pers. comm., April 2024).

In material terms, the LC I warrior burials and the bronze axes, belts and equid remains associated with them may be regarded as early material indicators of increasing mercantile contacts between Cyprus and the Levant (Steel 2013: 148–152). The built ashlar tombs of both Ugarit and Enkomi (LC II) — and perhaps the burial vaults off Courtyard II beneath the 'royal palace' at Ugarit (Yon 2006: 37 fig. 20, 40) — may have belonged to kin groups who identified themselves with an international merchant class linked not only through trading alliances but perhaps by marriage as well. In such a scenario, Keswani (2012: 198) suggested that members of these family groups who resided at both sites may have defined their material and social identities fluidly and contingently, adopting an international artistic style (Feldman 2002) in multiple types of media (including branded ingots), thus expressing shared social relationships. Although the Cypriot seals found at Ugarit cannot be linked definitively to Cypriot merchants, their contextual association with Ugaritic merchants such as Rap'ānu, Rašap-Abu and Urtenu suggests a vital, perhaps even familial commercial relationship (Smith 2022: 220). Moreover, the grand merchant houses of Ugarit now find their humbler equivalents at several key, mostly port sites on Cyprus (Hala Sultan Tekke, Kition, Maroni *Tsaroukkas*, Kalavasos *Ayios Dhimitrios* and Maa) (Knapp and Meyer 2023).

CHAPTER 8

Conclusions

By the end of the MC period (ca. 1650 BC) at the latest, some people from Cyprus began to enjoy close contacts with merchants, traders and elites in Levantine coastal sites, notably with those from Ugarit and its ports. Such contacts enabled Cypriots to acquire not only knowledge of distance and mercantile practices but also new material goods, both factors that could be parlayed into significant sources of power and prestige in their own, island context (Steel 2013: 155).

Owing at least in part to their geographic position, some Cypriot coastal polities and Levantine port towns like Ugarit would have hosted commercial sailing vessels (both heavily capitalised, large ships and smaller, private boats) deeply engaged in the exchange networks that underpinned maritime trade in the LBA eastern Mediterranean. The mercantile success of these communities surely resulted from the practical knowledge of their inhabitants, knowledge associated both with the goods they produced and with the ability to distribute those goods through maritime networks. Multiple texts from Ugarit support the contention that local mariners or merchants had the capital accumulation and technological know-how necessary to build the ships and maintain them in existing webs of exchange. The numerous ship models known from LBA Cyprus may suggest the same (summarised, with refs., in Knapp 2018: 141–144). Although Matoïan (2021c) discussed the rare ship's representations known from Ugarit, including an unpublished terracotta model (RS 8.275), she drew no wider conclusions about their economic or mercantile significance.

As this study has demonstrated, economic and social exchanges between Cyprus and Ugarit, the wider Levant, and beyond to Egypt, are well attested in a wide range of material and documentary evidence. Merchants, mariners and emissaries in all the polities involved would have been familiar with their foreign counterparts, and some certainly travelled to overseas destinations. Coastal ports on both Cyprus and in the Levant clearly were oriented towards the connecting sea: those on Cyprus were geared to answer foreign demand for copper and other manufactured goods, whilst those in the Levant — and in particular Ugarit — served as trading hubs on a much broader scale with a deeper time depth, and arguably with a more culturally embedded form of mercantile behavior, i.e., Monroe's (2015: 37–38) entrepreneurial sphere.

Kopytoff (1986: 67) argued that the significance of engaging with foreign objects or ideas lies not in their actual adoption, but in the ways they may be redefined culturally and put to use (see also Knapp 2006). Citing Kopytoff, Steel (2023: 187) recently observed that Mycenaean pictorial kraters depicting chariots, or their counterparts produced on Cyprus, may have been targeted at the Cypro-Ugaritic market. Susnow et al. (2024) have shown how local, Levantine potters (Tel Burna, Israel) adapted the concept, not the form, of imported Cypriot pithoi to produce local variants. Because all such objects moving between the Levant and Cyprus became integrated into new and different ways of life, they were transformed from a commodity into a new, socially desirable item embedded in new material and market conditions (Appadurai 1986: 15–16). The cultural biographies (Gosden and Marshall 1999) and social lives of all such objects were complex and frequently changed in meaning as they moved from Ugarit to Cyprus or vice-versa.

This study has tallied 670 Cypriot pottery vessels from various deposits at Ras Shamra, Minet el-Beidha and Ras Ibn Hani, and an estimated 350 CJs found at 21 different Middle and Late Bronze Age sites on Cyprus. The significance of these and all the other objects exchanged between Ugarit and Cyprus derives from the events and travels to which they were linked throughout their life histories and amongst the people who displayed or exchanged them. Key social objects in their own right, they were imbued with a past that linked their new owners to other élites in the eastern Mediterranean interaction sphere. The symbolism and status inherent in Levantine luxury objects or in the designs of Cypriot ceramics, metal products and seals found overseas formed key components in Bronze Age eastern Mediterranean networks of exchange. On Cyprus, the images that appeared on many of these items (e.g., chariots, leonine creatures, sphinxes, griffins) were unattested before the beginning of the LC period. The biographic aura embedded in such luxury goods offered Cypriot as well as Ugaritic élites a blueprint for power and authority, especially between themselves and the merchants and managers whose compliance and cooperation they sought. Perhaps we should envision all such elite objects, and the social practices facilitated by them, as 'calling cards' from one wealthy mercantile family to another, a type of social lubrication that enabled further self-enrichment and politico-economic power (Nathan Meyer, pers. comm., April 2024).

The level and material content of trade conducted between Cyprus and Ugarit seems to have remained constant between about 1500-1200 BC. The objects and ideologies of connectivity that characterised these exchanges formed an integral part of the cosmopolitan LBA eastern Mediterranean. The impression one gains from this study is that of two very different societies which shared a vital, commercial link, perhaps a 'brand community' if not an actual familial relationship. Ugaritic merchants operated out of a long-established trading emporium, whereas their Cypriot counterparts were evolving within a productive, island-based economy (raw materials first, finished goods later). In other words, from the more loosely formed society on Cyprus, one that was rapidly innovating in commercial enterprises, something new and distinct emerged (Knapp and Meyer 2023). Ugarit and the main Cypriot ports were very different places, and the vital commercial link they shared, over time, had a transformative impact on Cyprus.

REFERENCES

Åström, P., 1957. *The Middle Cypriote Bronze Age*. Lund: H. Ohlssons.

Åström, P., 1966. *Excavations at Kalopsidha and Ayios Iakovos in Cyprus*. Studies in Mediterranean Archaeology 2. Lund: P. Åström's Förlag.

Åström, P., 1972a. *The Late Cypriote Bronze Age. Architecture and Pottery*. The Swedish Cyprus Expedition IV: 1C. Lund: Swedish Cyprus Expedition.

Åström, P., 1972b. *The Middle Cypriote Bronze Age*. Swedish Cyprus Expedition IV: 1B. Lund: Swedish Cyprus Expedition.

Åström, P., 1986. Hala Sultan Tekke — an international harbour town of the Late Cypriote Bronze Age. *Opuscula Atheniensia* 16: 7–17.

Åström, P., 1989. *Hala Sultan Tekke 9: Trenches 1972-1987, with an Index for Volumes 1-9*. Studies in Mediterranean Archaeology 45.9. Göteborg: P. Åström's Förlag.

Åström, P., 1991a. Problems of definition of local and imported fabrics of Late Cypriot Canaanite ware. In J.A. Barlow, D. Bolger and B. Kling (eds), *Cypriot Ceramics: Reading the Prehistoric Record*. University Museum Monograph 74: 67–72. Philadelphia: University Museum, University of Pennsylvania.

Åström, P., 1991b. Canaanite jars from Hala Sultan Tekke. In N.H. Gale (ed.), *Bronze Age Trade in the Mediterranean*. Studies in Mediterranean Archaeology 90: 149–151. Göteborg: P. Åström's Förlag.

Åström, P., 2001. Bichrome hand-made ware and Bichrome wheel-made ware on Cyprus. In P. Åström (ed.), *The Chronology of Base-ring Ware and Bichrome Wheel-made Ware*. Konferenser 54: 131–142. Stockholm: Kungl. Vitterhets Historie och Antikvitets Akademien.

Åström, P., and E. Masson, 1982. A silver bowl from Hala Sultan Tekke. *Report of the Department of Antiquities, Cyprus*: 72–76.

Åström, P., D.M. Bailey and V. Karageorghis, 1976. *Hala Sultan Tekke* 1: *Excavations 1897-1971*. Studies in Mediterranean Archaeology 45.1. Göteborg: P. Åström's Förlag.

Akkermans, P.M.M.G., and G.M. Schwartz, 2003. *The Archaeology of Syria: From Complex Hunter-Gatherers to Early Urban Societies (ca. 16,000-300 BC)*. Cambridge: Cambridge University Press.

Al-Maqdissi, M., and V. Matoïan, 2008. La céramique découverte par C. Schaeffer dans le Palais royal d'Ougarit: remarques générales. In V. Matoïan (ed.), *Le mobilier du Palais royal d'Ougarit*. Ras Shamra-Ougarit 17: 127–155. Lyon: Maison de l'Orient et de la Méditerranée.

Alberti, M.E., and N. Parise, 2005. Towards a unification of mass-units between the Aegean and the Levant. In R. Laffineur and E. Greco (eds), *Emporia: Aegeans in the Central and Eastern Mediterranean*. Aegaeum 25 (1): 381–391. Liège, Austin: Université de Liège, University of Texas at Austin.

Amiet, P., 1992. *Corpus des cylindres de Ras Shamra-Ougarit* II: *Sceaux-cylindres en hematite et pierres diverses*. Ras Shamra-Ougarit 9. Paris: Éditions Recherche sur les Civilisations.

Amiran, R., 1970. *Ancient Pottery of the Holy Land*. New Brunswick, New Jersey: Rutgers University Press.

Andreou, G.M., 2016. Understanding the rural economy of Late Bronze Age Cyprus: a diachronic perspective from the Vasilikos Valley. *Journal of Mediterranean Archaeology* 29: 143–172.

Andreou, G.M., 2019. Socioeconomics of agrarian production: considering rural cooperatives in the archaeology of the eastern Mediterranean through the lens of 2nd millennium BCE Cyprus. *World Archaeology* 51: 291–310.

Andreou, G.M., A. Georgiou, T.W. Urban, K.D. Fisher, S.W. Manning and D.A. Sewell, 2019. Reconsidering coastal archaeological sites in Late Bronze Age Cyprus: Tochni *Lakkia* and the south-central coastscape. *Bulletin of the American Schools of Oriental Research* 382: 33–69.

Anson, D., 1980. Composition and provenance of Rude Style and related wares. *Report of the Department of Antiquities, Cyprus*: 109–127.

Antoniadou, S., 2005. The impact of trade on Late Cypriot society: a contextual study of imports from Enkomi. In J. Clarke (ed.), *Archaeological Perspectives on the Transmission and Transformation of Culture in the Eastern Mediterranean*, 66–77. Oxford: Oxbow.

Appadurai, A., 1986. Toward an anthropology of things. In A. Appadurai (ed.), *The Social Life of Things*, 3–63. Cambridge: Cambridge University Press.

Arnaud, D., 1984. La lettre Hani 81/4 et l'identification du site de Ras Ibn Hani. *Syria* 61: 15–23.

Arnaud, P., 2005. *Les routes de la navigation antique. Itinéraires en Méditerranée*. Paris: Errance.

Arnaud, P., 2011. Ancient sailing—routes and trade patterns: the impact of human factors. In D. Robinson and A. Wilson (eds), *Maritime Archaeology and Ancient Trade in the Mediterranean*. Oxford Centre for Maritime Archaeology, Monograph 6: 61–80. Oxford: Oxford Centre for Maritime Archaeology.

Artzy, M., 1973. The Late Bronze 'Palestinian' Bichrome Ware in its Cypriote context. In H.A. Hoffner, Jr. (ed.), *Orient and Occident*. Alter Orient und Altes Testament 22: 9–16. Neukirchen-Vluyn: Verlag Butzon and Bercker.

Artzy, M., 2001a. A study of the Cypriote Bichrome ware: past, present and future. In P. Åström (ed.), *The Chronology of Base-ring Ware and Bichrome Wheel-made Ware*. Konferenser 54: 154–174. Stockholm: Kungl. Vitterhets Historie och Antikvitets Akademien.

Artzy, M., 2001b. White Slip ware for export? The economics of production. In V. Karageorghis (ed.), *The White Slip Ware of Late Bronze Age Cyprus*. Österreichische Akademie der Wissenschaften, Denkschriften der Gesamtakademie Band 20. Contributions to the Chronology of the Eastern Mediterranean 2: 107–115. Vienna: Österreichische Akademie der Wissenschaften.

Artzy, M., 2002. The Aegean, Cyprus, the Levant and Bichrome Ware: eastern Mediterranean Middle Bronze Age koine? In E.D. Oren and S. Ahituv (eds), *Aharon Kempinski Memorial Volume: Studies in Archaeology and Related Disciplines*. Beer-Sheva 15: 1–20. Beersheva: Ben-Gurion University of Negev Press.

Artzy, M., and F. Asaro, 1979. Origin of Tell el-Yahudiyeh ware found in Cyprus. *Report of the Department of Antiquities, Cyprus*: 135–150.

Artzy, M., F. Asaro and I. Perlman, 1973. The origin of the Palestinian 'Bichrome' Ware. *Journal of the American Oriental Society* 93: 446–461.

Artzy, M., F. Asaro and I. Perlman, 1975. Consideration of the Tel Nagila Bichrome Ware krater as a Cypriot product. *Israel Exploration Journal* 25: 129–134.

Artzy, M., I. Perlman and F. Asaro, 1981. Cypriote pottery imports at Ras Shamra. *Israel Exploration Journal* 31: 37–47.

Aston, D.A., 2008. A history of Tell el-Yahudieh typology. In M. Bietak and E. Czerny (eds), *The Bronze Age in the Lebanon. Studies on the Archaeology and Chronology of Lebanon, Syria and Egypt*. Denkschrfiten der Gesamtakademie 50. Contributions to the Chronology of the Eastern Mediterranean 17: 165–194. Vienna: Österreichischen Akademie der Wissenschaften.

Aston, D.A., and M. Bietak, 2012. *The Classification and Chronology of Tell el-Yahudiya Ware*. Tell el-Dabʿa 8. Österreichische Akademie der Wissenschaften, Denkschriften der Gesamtakademie 66. Vienna: Österreichische Akademie der Wissenschaften,

Astour, M.C., 1970. Maʿhadu, the harbor of Ugarit. *Journal of the Economic and Social History of the Orient* 13: 113–127.

Astour, M.C., 1972. The merchant class of Ugarit. In D.O. Edzard (ed.), *Gesellschaftsklassen im Alten Zweistromland und in den angrenzenden Gebieten*. Rencontre Assyriologique Internationale 18. Abhandlungen der Bayerische Akademie der Wissenschaften 75: 11–26. Munich: Bayerische Akademie der Wissenschaften.

Atkins, C., 2022. Ceramics and stone anchors: re-assessing the anchorage at Maroni *Tsaroukkas*. In S.W. Manning (ed.), *Critical Approaches to Cypriot and Wider Mediterranean Archaeology*. Monographs in Mediterranean Archaeology 16: 296–312. Sheffield: Equinox.

Bar-Yosef Mayer, D., Y. Kahanov, J. Roskin and H. Gildor, 2015. Neolithic voyages to Cyprus: wind patterns, routes, and mechanisms. *Journal of Island and Coastal Archaeology* 10: 412–435.

Beckman, G. (ed.), 1996. *Hittite Diplomatic Texts*. SBL Writings from the Ancient World 7. Atlanta, Georgia: Scholars Press.

Bell, C., 2006. *The Evolution of Long Distance Trading Relationships across the LBA/Iron Age Transition on the North Levantine Coast*. British Archaeological Reports, International Series 1574. Oxford: Archaeopress.

Bell, C., 2012. The merchants of Ugarit: oligarchs of the Late Bronze Age trade in metals? In V. Kassianidou and G. Papasavvas (eds), *Eastern Mediterranean Metallurgy and Metalwork in the Second Millennium BC*, 180–187. Oxford: Oxbow.

Bergoffen, C.J., 2013. Red Lustrous Wheelmade and coarse-ware spindle bottles from Ashkelon. In R. B. Koehl (ed.), *Amilla. The Quest for Excellence. Studies Presented to Guenter Kopcke in Celebration of His 75th Birthday*. Prehistory Monographs 43: 281–292. Philadelphia: INSTAP Academic Press.

Bergoffen, C.J., 2018. Cypriot pottery found in Middle Bronze Age Ashkelon. In L.E. Stager, J.D. Schloen and R.J. Voss (eds), *The Middle Bronze Age Ramparts and Gates of the North Slope and Later Fortifications*. Ashkelon 6: 245–265. University Park, Pennsylvania: Eisenbrauns.

Bergoffen, C.J., 2023. The Middle to Late Bronze Age transition at Tell el- Ajjul in the light of exchanges between Cyprus and the eastern Mediterranean. In A. Hausleiter (ed.), *Material Worlds: Interdisciplinary Approaches to Contacts and Exchange in the Ancient Near East*, 45–51. Oxford: Archaeopress.

Bessac, J.-C., and V. Matoïan, 2020. Ashlar in Ras Shamra-Ugarit: uses, functions, and techniques. In M. Devolder and I. Kreimerman (eds), *ASHLAR: Exploring the Materiality of Cut-Stone Masonry in the Eastern Mediterranean Bronze Age*. Aegis 17: 265–306. Louvain-la-Neuve: Presses universitaires de Louvain.

Bevan, A., 2010. Making and marking relationships: Bronze Age brandings and Mediterranean commodities. In A. Bevan and D. Wengrow (eds), *Commodities of Cultural Branding*, 35–85. Walnut Creek, California: Left Coast Press.

Bevan, A., and D. Wengrow (eds), 2010. *Commodities of Cultural Branding*. Walnut Creek, California: Left Coast Press.

Bordreuil, P., 1983. Cunéiformes alphabétiques non canoniques. II. A propos de l'épigraphe de Hala Sultan Tekké. *Semitica* 33: 7–15.

Bordreuil, P. (ed.), 1991. *Une bibliothèque au sud de la ville. Les Textes de la 34e Campagne*. Ras Shamra-Ougarit 7. Paris: Éditions Recherche sur les Civilisations.

Bordreuil, P., 2007. Ugarit and the Bible: new data from the House of Urtenu. In K.L. Younger (ed.), *Ugarit at Seventy-Five*, 89–99. Winona Lake, Indiana: Eisenbrauns.

Bordreuil, P., and D. Pardee, 2004. *Manuel d'ougaritique 1. Grammaire, facsimilés*; 2. *Choix de textes, glossaire*. Paris: Geuthner.

Bordreuil, P., and D. Pardee, 2009. *Manuel d'Ougaritique II: Choix de textes, glossaire*. Paris: Geuthner.

Bordreuil, P., and F. Malbran-Labat, 1995. L'archives de la maison d'Ourtenou. *Academie des Inscriptions et Belles Lettres: Compete Rendus des Séances*: 443–449.

Bordreuil, P., D. Pardee and R. Hawley, 2012. *Une bibliothèque au sud de la ville***. Textes 1994–2002 en cunéiforme alphabétique de la Maison d'Ourtenu*. Ras Shamra-Ougarit 18. Lyon: La maison de l'Orient et de la Méditerranée Jean Pouilloux.

Bounni, A., 2000. The problem of the identification of the city on Ras Ibn Hani, Syria. In L.E. Stager, J.A. Greene and M.D. Coogan (eds), *The Archaeology of Jordan and Beyond: Essays in Honor of James A. Sauer*. Studies in the History and Archaeology of the Levant 1: 81–83. Winona Lake, Indiana: Eisenbrauns.

Bounni, A., E. Lagarce and J. Lagarce, 1998. *Ras Ibn Hani* I: *Le Palais Nord du Bronze Récent: Fouilles 1979-1995, Synthèse Préliminaire*. Bibliothèque Archéologique et Historique 151. Beirut: Institue Français d'Archéologie du Proche Orient.

Boyes, P.J., 2021. *Script and Society: The Social Context of Writing Practices in Late Bronze Age Ugarit*. Contexts of and Relations Between Early Writing Systems 3. Oxford: Oxbow.

Bretschneider, J., J. Driessen and A. Kanta, 2021. Cyprus and Ugarit at the end of the Late Bronze Age: insights from Pyla *Kokkinokremos*. In V. Matoïan (ed.), *Ougarit, un anniversaire. Bilans et recherches en cours*. Ras Shamra-Ougarit 28: 607–638. Louvain: Peeters.

Bretschneider, J., A. Kanta and J. Driessen, 2023. *Excavations at Pyla Kokkinokremos: Report on the 2014-2019 Campaigns*. Aegis 24. Louvain: Presses universitaires de Louvain.

Broodbank, C., 2010. 'Ships a-sail from over the rim of the sea': voyaging, sailing and the making of Mediterranean societies c. 3500-800 BC. In A. Anderson, J. Barrett and K. Boyle (eds.), *The Global Origins and Development of Seafaring*, 249–264. Cambridge: McDonald Institute for Archaeological Research.

Broodbank, C., 2013. *The Making of the Middle Sea: A History of the Mediterranean from the Beginning to the Emergence of the Classical World*. London: Thames and Hudson.

Buchholz, H.-G., 1973. Tamassos, Zypern, 1970-1972. *Archäologischer Anzeiger* (1973:3): 295–388.

Buchholz, H.-G., 1999. *Ugarit, Zypern und Agäis: Kulturbezeihungen im zweiten Jahrtausend v. Chr.* Alter Orient und Altes Testament 261. Münster: Ugarit-Verlag.

Bürge, T., 2021. Mortuary landscapes revisited: dynamics of insularity and connectivity in mortuary ritual, feasting and commemoration in Late Bronze Age Cyprus. *Religions* 12: 877. DOI:10.3390/rel12100877.

Bushnell, L., 2016. *Precious Commodities: The Socio-Economic Implications of the Distribution of Juglets in the Eastern Mediterranean during the Middle and Late Bronze Age*. British Archaeological Reports, International Series 2826. Oxford: BAR Publishing.

Cadogan, G., 1984. Maroni and the Late Bronze Age of Cyprus. In V. Karageorghis and J.D. Muhly (eds.), *Cyprus at the Close of the Late Bronze A*ge, 1–10. Nicosia: Leventis Foundation.

Cadogan, G., 1998. The thirteenth century changes in Cyprus in their eastern Mediterranean context. In S. Gitin, A. Mazar and E. Stern (eds), *Mediterranean Peoples in Transition: Thirteenth to Tenth Centuries BCE*, 6–16. Jerusalem: Israel Exploration Society.

Cadogan, G., E. Herscher, P. Russell and S.W. Manning, 2001. Maroni *Vournes*: a long White Slip sequence and its chronology. In V. Karageorghis (ed.), *The White Slip Ware of Late Bronze Age Cyprus*. Österreichische Akademie der Wissenschaften, Denkschriften der Gesamtakademie, Band 20. Contributions to the Chronology of the Eastern Mediterranean 2: 75–88. Vienna: Österreichische Akademie der Wissenschaften.

Callot, O., 1983. *Une maison à Ugarit: études d'architecture domestique*. Ras Shamra-Ougarit 1. Éditions Recherche sur les Civilisations, Memoire 28. Paris: ADPF.

Callot, O., 1994. *La tranchée 'Ville Sud': études d'architecture domestique*. Ras Shamra-Ougarit 10. Paris: Éditions Recherche sur les Civilisations.

Calvo Trias, M., and A. Galmés-Alba, 2024. Watching the horizon: coastal navigation strategies in the Balearic archipelago during the Middle and Late Bronze Ages. *Journal of Island and Coastal Archaeology*. DOI:10.1080/15564894.2024.2307370.

Cateloy, C., 2016. Trade and capacity studies in the eastern Mediterranean: the first Levantine trade amphorae. In S. Demesticha and A.B. Knapp (eds.), *Maritime Transport Containers in the Bronze-Iron Age Aegean and Eastern Mediterranean*. Studies in Mediterranean Archaeology and Literature, PB 183: 39–55. Uppsala: Åströms Förlag.

Catling, H.W., 1964. *Cypriot Bronzework in the Mycenaean World*. Oxford: Oxford University Press.

Catling, H.W., 1975. Cyprus in the Late Bronze Age. In I.E.S. Edwards, C.J. Gadd, N.G.L. Hammond and E. Sollberger (eds), *Cambridge Ancient History* II.2: 188–216. Cambridge: Cambridge University Press.

Catling, H.W., 1983. Review of E. Gjerstad, *Ages and Days in Cyprus* (Studies in Mediterranean Archaeology Pocket-book 12). *Antiquity* 57: 71–72.

Catling, H.W., 2020. *Kouklia: Late Bronze Age and Early Iron Age Tombs at Palaepaphos 1951-1954. Excavations of the Liverpool City Museum and St Andrews University Expedition to Palaepaphos*. British Archaeological Reports, International Series 2994. Oxford: BAR Publishing.

Caubet, A., 2009. A tale of two cities. Le coffre en ivoire d'Enkomi et la couple d'or d'Ougarit. In T. Kiely (ed.), *Ancient Cyprus in the British Museum: Essays in Honour of Dr Veronica Tatton-Brown*. British Museum Press Research Publication 180: 57–62. London: British Museum.

Caubet, A., and F. Poplin, 1992. La place des ivoires d'Ougarit dans la production du Proche Orient ancien. In J.L. Fitton (ed.), *Ivory in Greece and the Eastern Mediterranean, from the Bronze Age to the Hellenistic Period*. British Museum Occasional Paper 85: 91–100. London: British Museum Publications.

Caubet, A., and M. Yon. 2001. Une coupe inscrite en chypro-minoen à Ras Shamra et les 'trésors' d'Ougarit. In P.M. Fischer (ed.), *Contributions to the Archaeology and History of the Bronze and Iron Ages in the Eastern Mediterranean: Studies in Honour of Paul Åström*. Österreichisches Archäologisches Institut, Sonderschriften Band 39: 149–157. Vienna: Österreichisches Archäologisches Institut.

Chanut, C., 2000. Bois, pierres et métaux à Ugarit-Ras Shamra (Syrie) à l'âge du Bronze Récent, d'après les données des sciences naturelles, de l'archéologie et des textes. Lille: Atelier National de Reproduction des Thèses.

Charaf, H., 2010-11. Cypriot imported pottery from the Middle Bronze Age in Lebanon. *Berytus* 53-54: 147–165.

Charalambous, A., V. Kassianidou and G. Papasavvas, 2014. A compositional study of Cypriot bronzes dating to the early Iron Age using portable X-ray fluorescence spectrometry (pXRF). *Journal of Archaeological Science* 46: 205–216.

Cifola, B., 1994. The role of the Sea Peoples and the end of the Late Bronze Age: a reassessment of textual and archaeological evidence. *Orientis Antiqui Miscellanea* 1: 1–23.

Clark, B., 2024a. Cypriot connections through the Middle to Late Bronze Age in the western Galilee: a review of residual Cypriot pottery from Tel Achziv. In T. Bürge and L. Recht (eds), *Dynamics and Developments of Social Structures and Networks in Prehistoric and Protohistoric Cyprus*, 150–178. London, New York: Routledge.

Clark, B., 2024b. Cypriot pottery as an indicator of adaptive trade networks. In A. Yasur-Landau, G. Gambash and T.E. Levy (eds), *Mediterranean Resilience: Collapse and Adaptation in Antique Maritime Societies*, 92–114. Sheffield: Equinox.

Cohen, Y., 2021. The 'hunger years' and the 'sea peoples': preliminary observations on the recently published letters from the 'House of Urtenu' archive at Ugarit. In P. Machinist, R.A. Harris, Y. Berman, N. Samet and N. Ayali-Darshan (eds), *Ve-'Ed Ya'aleh (Gen 2:6): Essays in Biblical and Near Eastern Studies Presented to Edward L. Greenstein*. Writings from the Ancient World, Supplement Series 5: 47–62. Atlanta, Georgia: SBL Press.

Collard, D., 2008. *Function and Ethnicity: 'Bathtubs' from Late Bronze Age Cyprus*. Studies in Mediterranean Archaeology and Literature, Pocket-book 171. Sävedalen, Sweden: P. Åström's Förlag.

Constantinou, G., 1982. Geological features and ancient exploitation of the cupriferous sulphide orebodies of Cyprus. In J.D. Muhly, R. Maddin and V. Karageorghis (eds), *Early Metallurgy in Cyprus, 4000-500 BC*, 3–24. Nicosia: Pierides Foundation.

Courbin, P., 1986. Bassit. *Syria* 63: 175–220.

Courtois, J.-C., 1969. Enkomi-Alasia: glorious capital of Cyprus. *Archaeologia Viva* 1(3): 93–100.

Courtois, J.-C., 1971. Le sanctuaire du dieu au lingot d'Enkomi-Alasia. In C.F. A. Schaeffer (ed.), *Alasia* I. Mission Archéologique d'Alasia 4: 151–362. Paris: Klincksieck.

Courtois, J.-C., 1976. L'industrie du bronze à Ugarit (Syrie du nord) à l'age du Bronze Récent et ses prolongements à Chypre à l'époque de transition Bronze/Fer. In H. Muller-Karpe (ed.), *Jahresbericht des Instituts fur Vorgeschichte der Universitat Frankfurt am Mainz* 1975, 24–32. Munich: Verlag C.H. Beck.

Courtois, J.-C., 1979. Ras Shamra: archéologie. In H. Cazelles and A. Feuillet (eds), *Supplement au Dictionnaire de la Bible*, 1126–1295. Paris: ANE.

Courtois, J.-C., 1981. *Alasia* II. *Les tombes d'Enkomi. Le mobilier funéraire*. Mission Archéologique d'Alasia 5. Paris: Diffusion de Boccard.

Courtois, J.-C., 1986. À propos des apports orientaux dans la civilisation du Bronze Récent à Chypre. In V. Karageorghis (ed.), *Acts of the International Archaeological Symposium: Cyprus between the Orient and Occident*, 69–90. Nicosia: Department of Antiquities.

Courtois, J.-C., 1990. Yabninu et le palais sud d'Ougarit. *Syria* 67: 103–142.

Courtois, J.-C., and L. Courtois, 1978. Corpus céramique de Ras Shamra-Ugarit, niveau historique. Deuxième partie. In C.F.A. Schaeffer, *Ugartica* 7. Mission de Ras Shamra 18. Bibliothèque Archéologique et Historique 99: 191–370. Paris: Geuthner.

Courtois, J.-C., J. Lagarce and E. Lagarce, 1986. *Enkomi et le Bronze Récent à Chypre*. Nicosia: Leventis Foundation.

Crewe, L., 2007. *Early Enkomi. Regionalism, Trade and Society at the Beginning of the Late Bronze Age on Cyprus.* British Archaeological Reports, International Series 1706. Oxford: Archaeopress.

Crewe, L., 2009. Feasting with the dead? Tomb 66 at Enkomi. In T. Kiely (ed.), *Ancient Cyprus in the British Museum: Essays in Honour of Dr Veronica Tatton-Brown.* British Museum Press Research Publication 180: 26–48. London: British Museum.

Crewe, L., 2010. Rethinking Kalopsidha: from specialisation to state marginalisation. In D. Bolger and L.C. Maguire (eds.), *The Development of Pre-State Communities in the Ancient Near East.* BANEA Publication Series 2: 63–71. Oxford: Oxbow.

Crewe, L., 2012. Beyond copper: commodities and values in Middle Bronze Cypro-Levantine exchanges. *Oxford Journal of Archaeology* 31: 225–243.

Dardaillon, E., 2006. Les productions métalliques dans les royaumes du Levant au IIe millénaire av. J.-C. Unpublished PhD thesis, Université Lumière Lyon 2.

Dardaillon, E., 2008. Analyses métallurgiques. In Y. Calvet et M. Yon (eds.) *Ougarit: Au Bronze Moyen et au Bronze Récent.* Travaux de la Maison de l'Orient et de la Méditerranée 47: 159–168. Lyon: Maison de l'Orient et de la Méditerranée.

Dardaillon, E., 2012. The evidence for metallurgical workshops of the 2nd millennium in Ugarit. In V. Kassianidou and G. Papasavvas (eds), *Eastern Mediterranean Metallurgy and Metalwork in the Second Millennium BC*, 169–179. Oxford: Oxbow.

Davis, B., J. Maran and S. Wirghová, 2014. A new Cypro-Minoan inscription from Tiryns: TIRY Avas 002. *Kadmos* 53: 91–109.

Day, P.M., A. Hein, E. Kardamaki, J. Maran, M. Tenconi and P. Waiman-Barak, 2020. Maritime commodity trade from the Near East to the Mycenaean heartland: Canaanite jars in Final Palatial Tiryns. *Jahrbuch des Deutschen Archäologischen Instituts* 135: 1–99.

del Olmo Lete, G., 2018. *The Private Archives of Ugarit. A Functional Analysis.* Barcino Monographica Orientalia 11. Barcelona: University of Barcelona.

Demesticha, S., 2022. Seascapes and maritime capacity of Late Roman Cyprus. In S.W. Manning (ed.), *Critical Approaches to Cypriot and Wider Mediterranean Archaeology.* Monographs in Mediterranean Archaeology 16: 313–340. Sheffield: Equinox.

Dietrich, M., 2000. Zypern und die Ägäis nach den Texten aus Ugarit. In S. Rogge (ed.), *Zypern–Insel im Brennpunkt der Kulturen.* Schriften des Instituts für Interdisziplinäre Zypern-Studien 1: 70–89. Münster: Waxmann.

Dietrich, M., and O. Loretz, 1969. Beschriftete Lungen- und Leber-Modelle aus Ugarit. In C.F.A. Schaeffer (ed.), *Ugaritica* 6. Mission de Ras Shamra 17, Bibliothèque Archéologique et Historique 81: 165–179. Paris: Geuthner.

Dietrich, M., and O. Loretz, 1978. Der 'Seefahrende Volk' von Sikila (RS 34.129). *Ugarit-Forschungen* 10: 53–56.

Dietrich, M., O. Loretz and J. Sanmartín, 2013. *Die keilalphabetischen Texte aus Ugarit, Ras Ibn Hani und anderen Orten.* 3rd ed. Alter Orient und Altes Testament 360.1. Münster: Ugarit Verlag.

Dikaios, P., 1969-1971. *Enkomi. Excavations 1948-1958.* 3 volumes. Mainz-am-Rhein: Philip von Zabern.

Donnelly, C., 2022. Cypro-Minoan and its potmarks and vessel inscriptions as challenges to Aegean scripts corpora. In P.M. Steele and P.J. Boyes (eds), *Writing Around the Ancient Mediterranean: Practices and Adaptations*. Contexts of and Relations between Early Writing Systems 6: 49–73. Oxford: Oxbow.

Duhoux, Y., 2013. Non-Greek languages of ancient Cyprus and their scripts: Cypro-Minoan 1–3. In P.M. Steele (ed.), *Syllabic Writing on Cyprus and its Context*, 27–48. Cambridge: Cambridge University Press.

du Plat Taylor, J., 1952. A Late Bronze Age settlement at Apliki, Cyprus. *Antiquaries Journal* 32: 133–167.

du Plat Taylor, J., 1957. *Myrtou-Pighades: A Late Bronze Age Sanctuary in Cyprus*. Oxford: Ashmolean Museum.

Egetmeyer, M., 2013. Ougarit et le déchiffrement de ses inscriptions in syllabaire chypro-minoen. In P. Bordreuil, F. Ernst-Pradal, M.G. Masetti-Rouault, H. Rouillard-Bonraisin and M. Zink (eds), *Les écritures mises au jour sur le site antique d'Ougarit (Syrie) et leur déchiffrement, 1930-2010: commémoration du quatre-vingtième anniversaire du déchiffrement de l'alphabet cunéiforme de Ras Shamra-Ougarit*, 135–155. Paris: Académie des Inscriptions et Belles-Lettres.

Epstein, C., 1966. *Palestinian Bichrome Ware*. Leiden: Brill.

Feldman, M.H., 2002. Luxurious forms: redefining a Mediterranean 'International Style', 1400-1200 B.C.E. *Art Bulletin* 84: 6–29.

Feldman, M.H., 2006. *Diplomacy by Design: Luxury Arts and an 'International Style' in the Ancient Near East, 1400-1200 BC*. Chicago: University of Chicago Press.

Feldman, M.H., and C. Sauvage, 2010. Objects of prestige? Chariots in the Late Bronze Age eastern Mediterranean and Near East. *Ägypten und Levante* 20: 67–181.

Ferrara, S., 2009. Writing without reading. The Cypro-Minoan script between the Linear and the cuneiform traditions. *Bulletin of the Institute of Classical Studies* 52: 259–260.

Ferrara, S., 2012. *Cypro Minoan Inscriptions* 1: *Analysis*. Oxford: Oxford University Press.

Ferrara, S., 2015. The royal and the layman? Possible onomastics on Late Bronze Age clay balls. *Studi Micenei ed Egeo-Anatolici* n.s.1: 105–115.

Ferrara, S., 2016. Writing away: mobility and versatility of scribes at the end of the Late Bronze Age. *Oxford Journal of Archaeology* 35: 227–245.

Fischer, P.M., 1991. Canaanite pottery from Hala Sultan Tekke: analysis with secondary ion mass spectrometry. In N.H. Gale (ed.), *Bronze Age Trade in the Mediterranean*. Studies in Mediterranean Archaeology 90: 152–161. Göteborg: P. Åström's Förlag.

Fischer, P.M., and T. Bürge, 2018. *Two Late Cypriot City Quarters at Hala Sultan Tekke. The Söderberg Expedition 2010–2017*. Studies in Mediterranean Archaeology 147. Uppsala: Åström Editions.

Fischer, P.M., and T. Bürge, 2021. The New Swedish Cyprus Expedition 2020 (The Söderberg Expedition): excavations in the cemetery of Hala Sultan Tekke. *Ägypten und Levante* 31: 97–145.

Fischer, P.M., and T. Bürge, 2022. The New Swedish Cyprus Expedition (The Söderberg Expedition): excavations at Hala Sultan Tekke 2020 and 2021. *Opuscula* 15: 7–76.

Fisher, K.D., 2020. The materiality of ashlar masonry on Late Bronze Age Cyprus. In M. Devolder and I. Kreimerman (eds), *ASHLAR: Exploring the Materiality of Cut-Stone Masonry in the Eastern Mediterranean Bronze Age*. Aegis 17: 307–339. Louvain-la-Neuve: Presses universitaires de Louvain.

Fisher, K.D., 2023. *Monumentality, Place-making, and Social Interaction on Late Bronze Age Cyprus*. Monographs in Mediterranean Archaeology 17. Sheffield: Equinox.

Frost, H., 1963. From rope to chain: on the development of the anchor in the Mediterranean. *Mariner's Mirror* 49: 1–20.

Frost, H., 1969. The stone anchors of Ugarit. In C.F.A. Schaeffer (ed.), *Ugaritica* 6. Mission de Ras Shamra 17, Bibliothèque Archéologique et Historique 81: 235–245. Paris: Geuthner.

Frost, H., 1970. Bronze Age stone anchors from the eastern Mediterranean. *Mariner's Mirror* 56: 377–394.

Frost, H., 1972. Ancient harbours and anchorages in the eastern Mediterranean. In *Underwater Archaeology: A Nascent Discipline*. Museums and Monuments 13: 95–114. London and Paris: UNESCO.

Frost, H., 1985. The Kition anchors. Appendix I in V. Karageorghis and M. Demas, *Excavations at Kition* V.1: 281–321. Nicosia: Department of Antiquities.

Frost, H., 1991. Anchors sacred and profane. Ugarit-Ras Shamra 1986: the stone anchors revised and compared. In M. Yon (ed.), *Ras Shamra-Ougarit* 6: *Arts et Industries de la Pierre*, 355–408. Paris: Éditions Recherches sur les Civilisations/ADPF.

Frost, H., 1993. Stone anchors: a reassessment reassessed. *Mariner's Mirror* 79: 449–458.

Frost, H., 2004. Byblos and the sea. In C. Doumet-Serhal (ed.), *Decade: A Decade of Archaeology and History in the Lebanon*, 316–347. Beirut: Lebanese British Friends of the National Museum.

Gal, D., H. Saaroni and D. Cvikel, 2023. Mappings of potential sailing mobility in the Mediterranean during Antiquity. *Journal of Archaeological Method and Theory* 30: 397–448.

Gale, N.H., 1991. Copper oxhide ingots and their relation to the Bronze Age metals trade. In N.H. Gale (ed.), *Bronze Age Trade in the Mediterranean*. Studies in Mediterranean Archaeology 90: 197–239. Göteborg: P. Åström's Förlag.

Galili, E., and B. Rosen, 2015. Protecting the ancient mariners: cultic artifacts from the Holy Land seas. *Archaeologia Maritima Mediterranea* 12: 35–101.

Georgiadou, A., and A. Georgiou, 2019. Spinning, weaving and purple dyeing at Kition: new evidence for the textile industry at the settlement of Bamboula during the Late Bronze-Early Iron Age. *Cahiers du Centre d'Études Chypriotes* 49: 103–128.

Georgiou, A., 2014. The Canaanite jars. Appendix III in V. Karageorghis and A. Kanta, *Pyla-Kokkinokremos: A Late 13th Century BC Fortified Settlement in Cyprus. Excavations 2010-2011*. Studies in Mediterranean Archaeology 141: 175–187. Uppsala: Åström Editions.

Georgiou, A., 2018a. From the hand to the wheel: revisiting the transformations of the Late Cypriot ceramic industry of finewares during the 13th-to-12th c. BC transition. In I. Caloi and C. Langohr (eds), *Technology in Crisis. Technological Changes in Ceramic Production during Periods of Trouble*. Aegis 16: 177–200. Louvain: Presses universitaires de Louvain.

Georgiou, A., 2018b. Ceramic fluidity and regional variations: elucidating the transformed ceramic industry in Cyprus at the close of the Late Bronze Age. In A. Cannavò and L. Thély (eds), *Les royaumes de Chypre à l'épreuve de l'histoire: transitions et ruptures de la fin de l'âge du Bronze au début de l'époque hellénistique.* Bulletin de Correspondance Hellénique, Supplément 60: 29–48. Athens: École française d'Athènes.

Georgiou, A., 2024. Pursuits of social status and power at Maa *Paleokastro*. In T. Bürge and L. Recht (eds), *Dynamics and Developments of Social Structures and Networks in Prehistoric and Protohistoric Cyprus,* 255–280. London, New York: Routledge.

Georgiou, A., A. Georgiadou and S. Fourrier, 2022-23. Traditions and innovations during the 12th-to-11th century BC transition in Cyprus: new data from Kition *Bamboula. Cahiers du Centre d'Études Chypriote*s 52-53: 117–151.

Georgiou, G., 2009. The dynamism of central Cyprus during Middle Cypriot III: funerary evidence from Nicosia *Agia Paraskevi*. In I. Hein (ed.), *The Formation of Cyprus in the Second Millennium BC: Studies in Regionalism during the Middle and Late Bronze Ages.* Österreichische Akademie der Wissenschaften, Denkschriften der Gesamtakademie 52: 65–78. Vienna: Österreichische Akademie der Wissenschaften.

Gjerstad, E., 1926. *Studies on Prehistoric Cyprus.* Uppsala: Uppsala Universitets Arsskrift.

Goiran, J.-P., N. Marriner, B. Geyer, D. Laisney and V. Matoïan, 2015. Ras ibn Hani: "l'île" d'Ougarit. In B. Geyer, V. Matoïan and M. Al-Maqdissi (eds), *De l'île d'Aphrodite au Paradis perdu, itinéraire d'un gentilhomme lyonnais, en hommage à Yves Calvet.* Ras Shamra-Ougarit 22: 51–62. Leuven: Peeters.

Goren, Y., 2013. International exchange during the late second millennium BC: microarchaeological study of finds from the Uluburun ship. In J. Aruz, S.B. Graf and Y. Rakic (eds), *Cultures in Contact: From Mesopotamia to the Mediterranean in the Second Millennium BC,* 54–61. New York: Metropolitan Museum of Art.

Goren, Y., S. Bunimovitz, I. Finkelstein and N. Na'aman, 2003. The location of *Alashiya*: new evidence from petrographic investigation of *Alashiyan* tablets from el-Amarna and Ugarit. *American Journal of Archaeology* 107: 233–255.

Goren, Y., and A. Cohen-Weinberger, 2002. Petrographic analyses of selected wares. In A. Kempınski (ed.), *Tel Kabri. The 1986-1993 Excavation Seasons.* Sonia and Marco Nadler Institute of Archaeology, Monograph Series 20: 435–442. Tel Aviv: Institute of Archaeology, Tel Aviv University.

Goren, Y., I. Finkelstein and N. Na'aman, 2004. *Inscribed in Clay: Provenance Study of the Amarna Tablets and Other Ancient Near Eastern Texts.* Sonia and Marco Nader Institute of Archaeology, Monograph Series 23. Tel Aviv: Institute of Archaeology, Tel Aviv University.

Gosden, C., and Y. Marshall, 1999. The cultural biography of objects. *World Archaeology* 31: 169–178.

Grace, V., 1956. The Canaanite jar. In S. Weinberg (ed.), *The Aegean and the Near East: Studies Presented to Hetty Goldman,* 80–109. Locust Valley, New York: J.J. Augustin.

Graziadio, G., 2014. The oxhide ingots production in the eastern Mediterranean. *Egitto e Vicono Oriente* 37: 5–25.

Griffiths, D., 2011-12. Petrographic analysis of Tell el-Yahudiyeh ceramics. *Archaeology and History in the Lebanon* 34-35: 154–162.

Gunneweg, J., I. Perlman and F. Asaro, 1987. A Canaanite jar from Enkomi. *Israel Exploration Journal* 37: 168–172.

Güterbock, H.G., 1967. The Hittite conquest of Cyprus reconsidered. *Journal of Near Eastern Studies* 26: 73–81.

Hadjicosti, M., 1988. 'Canaanite' jars from Maa-*Palaeokastro*. In V. Karageorghis and M. Demas, *Excavations at Maa-Palaeokastro 1979-1986*, 340–385. Nicosia: Cyprus Department of Antiquties.

Hadjisavvas, S., 2017. *Alassa: Excavations at the Late Bronze Age sites of Pano Mandilares and Paliotaverna 1984-2000*. Nicosia: Cyprus Department of Antiquities.

Hameeuw, H., and G. Jans, 2008. Burial customs at Tell Tweini: Field A. In J. Bretschneider and K. Van Lerberghe (eds), *In Search of Gibala: An Archaeological and Historical Study Based on Eight Seasons of Excavations at Tell Tweini (Syria) in the A and C Fields (1999-2007)*. Aula Orientalis, Supplementa 24: 75–86. Barcelona: Sabadell, Editorial AUSA.

Hankey, V., 1967. Mycenaean pottery in the Middle East: notes on finds since 1951. *Annual of the British School at Athens* 62: 107–147.

Harpster, M., 2013. Shipwreck identity, methodology, and nautical archaeology. *Journal of Archaeological Method and Theory* 20: 588–622.

Hawley, R., D. Pardee and C. Roche, 2015. The scribal culture of Ugarit. *Journal of Ancient Near Eastern History* 2: 229–267.

Herdner, A., 1963. *Corpus des tablettes en cunéiformes alphabétiques découvertes à Ras Shamra-Ugarit de 1929 à 1939*. Mission de Ras Shamra 10. Paris: Klincksieck.

Hirschfeld, N., 2000. Marked Late Bronze Age pottery from the kingdom of Ugarit. In M. Yon, V. Karageorghis and N. Hirschfeld, *Céramiques mycéniennes d'Ougarit*. Ras Shamra-Ougarit 13: 163–200. Paris, Nicosia: ADPF, Leventis Foundation.

Hirschfeld, N., 2004. Eastward via Cyprus? The marked Mycenaean pottery of Enkomi, Ugarit and Tell Abu Hawam. In J. Balensi, J.-Y. Monchambert and S. Müller-Celku (eds), *La Céramique Mycénienne de l'Egée au Levant*. Travaux de la Maison de l'Orient 41: 97–103. Lyon: Travaux de la Maison de l'Orient.

Hirschfeld, N., 2009. The many ways between Late Bronze Age Aegeans and Levants. *BAAL Hors-Série* 6: 285–294.

Hirschfeld, N., 2014. Marked pottery at Pyla *Kokkinokremos*. Appendix II in V. Karageorghis and A. Kanta, *Pyla-Kokkinokremos: A Late 13th Century BC Fortified Settlement in Cyprus. Excavations 2010-2011*. Studies in Mediterranean Archaeology 141: 169–173. Uppsala: Åström Editions.

Hirschfeld, N., and G.F. Bass, 2013. Return to Cape Gelidonya. *Pasiphae* 7: 99–104.

Hitchcock, L., 2008. 'Do you see a man skillful in his work? He will stand before kings': interpreting the spread of architectural influences in the Bronze Age eastern Mediterranean. *Ancient West and East* 7: 17–49.

Höflmayer, F., H. Misgav, L. Webster and K. Streit, 2021. Early alphabetic writing in the ancient Near East: the 'missing link' from Tel Lachish. *Antiquity* 95/381: 705–719.

Howitt-Marshall, D., 2012. The anchorage site at Kouklia *Achni*, southwest Cyprus: problems and perspectives. In A. Georgiou (ed.), *Cyprus, An Island Culture: Society and Social Relations from the Bronze Age to the Venetian Period*, 104–121. Oxford: Oxbow.

Hult, G., 1983. *Bronze Age Ashlar Masonry in the Eastern Mediterranean: Cyprus, Ugarit, and Neighbouring Regions*. Studies in Mediterranean Archaeology 66. Göteborg: P. Åström's Förlag.

Hult, G., 1992. Nitovikla reconsidered. In P. Åström (ed.), *Acta Cypria* 2. Studies in Mediterranean Archaeology and Literature, Pocketbook 117: 165–170. Jonsered, Sweden: P. Åström's Förlag.

Iacovou, M., 1988. *The Pictorial Pottery of Eleventh Century BC Cyprus*. Studies in Mediterranean Archaeology 79. Göteborg: P. Åström's Förlag.

Ioannides, D., V. Kassianidou and G. Papasavvas, 2024. One city to rule them all? The production of copper in Enkomi, Cyprus: the evidence from the metallurgical ceramic assemblage. *Research Square* (preliminary report without peer review). DOI:10.21203/rs.3.rs-4313680/v1.

Jacobs, A., 2016. The Plain and Canaanite wares. In C. von Rüden, A. Georgiou, A. Jacobs and P. Halstead, *Feasting, Craft and Depositional Practice in Late Bronze Age Palaepaphos. The Well Fillings of Evreti*. Bochumer Forschungen zur Ur- und Frühgeschichtlichen Archäologie 8: 39–70. Rahden-Westfallen, Germany: Verlag Marie Leidorf GmbH.

Jansen, M., A. Hauptmann, S. Klein and H.M. Seitz, 2018. The potential of stable Cu isotopes for the identification of Bronze Age ore mineral sources from Cyprus and Faynan: results from Uluburun and Khirbat Hamra Ifdan. *Archaeological and Anthropological Sciences* 10: 1485–1502.

Jones, R.E., and H.W. Catling, 1986. Cyprus, 2500-500 BC: the Aegean and the Near East, 1500-1050 BC. In R.E. Jones, *Greek and Cypriot Pottery: A Review of Scientific Studies*. Fitch Laboratory Occasional Paper 1: 523–625. Athens: British School at Athens.

Jones, R.E., and S.J. Vaughan, 1988. Part 2: A study of some 'Canaanite' jar fragments from Maa *Palaeokastro* by petrographic and chemical analysis. In V. Karageorghis and M. Demas, *Excavations at Maa-Palaeokastro 1979-1986*, 386–398. Nicosia: Cyprus Department of Antiquities.

Jung, R., H. Mommsen and T. Pedrazzi, 2023. The external contacts of Cyprus in the Late Bronze Age on the basis of the ceramic evidence. In T. Bürge and P.M. Fischer (eds), *The Decline of Bronze Age Civilisations in the Mediterranean: Cyprus and Beyond*. Studies in Mediterranean Archaeology 154: 137–199. Nicosia: Åstrom Editions.

Junker, L.L., 1999. *Raiding, Trading, and Feasting: The Political Economy of Philippine Chiefdoms*. Honolulu: University of Hawai'i Press.

Kaplan, M., 1980. *The Origin and Distribution of Tell Yahudiyeh Ware*. Studies in Mediterranean Archaeology 62. Göteborg: P. Åström's Förlag.

Karageorghis, V., 1990. *Tombs at Palaepaphos: 1) Teratsoudhia; 2) Eliomylia*. Nicosia: Leventis Foundation.

Karageorghis, V., 2001. Bichrome wheel-made ware: still a problem? In P. Åström (ed.), *The Chronology of Base-ring Ware and Bichrome Wheel-made Ware*. Konferenser 54: 143–155. Stockholm: Kungl. Vitterhets Historie och Antikvitets Akademien.

Karageorghis, V., and M. Demas, 1984. *Pyla-Kokkinokremos: A Late 13th Century B.C. Fortified Settlement in Cyprus*. Nicosia: Department of Antiquities, Cyprus.

Karageorghis, V., and M. Demas, 1985. *Excavations at Kition* V, Parts 1, 2. *The Pre-Phoenician Levels*. Nicosia: Department of Antiquities, Cyprus.

Karageorghis, V., and M. Demas, 1988. *Excavations at Maa Palaeokastro 1979-1986*. Nicosia: Department of Antiquities, Cyprus.

Karageorghis, V., and A. Kanta, 2014. *Pyla-Kokkinokremos: A Late 13th Century BC Fortified Settlement in Cyprus. Excavations 2010-2011*. Studies in Mediterranean Archaeology 141. Uppsala: Åström Editions.

Kassianidou, V., 2003. The trade of tin and the island of copper. In A. Giumlia-Mair and F. Lo Schiavo (eds), *The Problem of Early Tin*. British Archaeological Reports, International Series 1199: 109–119. Oxford: Archaeopress.

Kassianidou, V., 2008. The formative years of the Cypriot copper industry. In I. Tzachili (ed.), *Aegean Metallurgy in the Bronze Age*, 249–267. Rethymnon, Crete: Ta Pragmata.

Kassianidou, V., 2009. Oxhide ingots in Cyprus. In F. Lo Schiavo, J. D. Muhly, R. Maddin and A. Giumlia Mair (eds), *Oxhide Ingots in the Central Mediterranean*, 41–81. Rome: Leventis Foundation, INSTAP, Consiglio Nazionale delle Ricerche.

Kassianidou, V., 2012. Metallurgy and metalwork in Enkomi: the early phases. In V. Kassianidou and G. Papasavvas (eds), *Eastern Mediterranean Metallurgy and Metalwork in the Second Millennium BC*, 94–106. Oxford: Oxbow.

Kassianidou, V., 2013. The production and trade of Cypriot copper in the Late Bronze Age. An analysis of the evidence. *Pasiphae* 7: 133–146.

Kassianidou, V., 2018. Apliki *Karamallos* on Cyprus: the 13th century BCE miners' settlement in context. In E. Ben-Yosef (ed.), *Mining for Ancient Copper. Essays in Memory of Beno Rothenberg*. Sonia and Marco Nadler Institute of Archaeology Monograph Series 37: 345–356. Tel Aviv: Nadler Institute of Archaeology, Tel Aviv University.

Kassianidou, V., 2022. Placing Politiko *Phorades* in the historiography and evolution of Late Cypriot metallurgy. In S.W. Manning (ed.), *Critical Approaches to Cypriot and Wider Mediterranean Archaeology*. Monographs in Mediterranean Archaeology 16: 87–107. Sheffield: Equinox.

Kassianidou, V., 2023. Early types of Cypriot Bronze Age metal ingots. In E. Ben-Yosef and I.W.N. Jones (eds), *"And in Length of Days Understanding" (Job 12:12). Essays on Archaeology in the Eastern Mediterranean and Beyond in Honor of Thomas E. Levy*, 1323–1354. Cham, Switzerland: Springer.

Keswani, P.S., 1989. Dimensions of social hierarchy in Late Bronze Age Cyprus: an analysis of the mortuary data from Enkomi. *Journal of Mediterranean Archaeology* 2: 49–86.

Keswani, P.S., 2004. *Mortuary Ritual and Society in Bronze Age Cyprus*. Monographs in Mediterranean Archaeology 9. London: Equinox.

Keswani, P.S., 2012. Urban mortuary practices at Enkomi and Ugarit in the second millennium BC. In P. Pfälzner, J. Niehr, E. Pernicka and A. Wissing (eds), *(Re-)Constructing Funerary Rituals in the Ancient Near East*. Qatna Studien Supplementa 1: 183–203. Wiesbaden: Harrassowitz.

Kibaroğlu, M., E. Kozal, A. Klügel, G. Hartmann and P. Monien, 2019. New evidence on the provenance of Red Lustrous Wheel-made Ware (RLW): petrographic, elemental and Sr-Nd isotope analysis. *Journal of Archaeological Science, Reports* 24: 412–433.

Killebrew, A., 2007. The Canaanite storage jar revisited. In S.W. Crawford, A. Ben-Tor, J.P. Dessel, W.G. Dever, A. Mazar and J. Aviram (eds), *"Up to the gates of Ekron": Essays on the Archaeology and History of the Eastern Mediterranean in Honor of Seymour Gitin*, 166–188. Jerusalem: Albright institute of Archaeological Research, Israel Exploration Society.

Kling, B., 1989. *Mycenaean IIIC:1b and Related Pottery in Cyprus*. Studies in Mediterranean Archaeology 87. Göteborg: P. Åström's Förlag.

Kling, B., 2000. Mycenaean IIIC:1b and related pottery in Cyprus: comments on the current state of research. In Eliezer D. Oren (ed.), *The Sea Peoples and Their World: A Reassessment*. University Museum Monograph 108, University Museum Symposium Series 11: 281–295. Philadelphia: University Museum, University of Pennsylvania.

Kling, B., and J.D. Muhly, 2007. *Joan du Plat Taylor's Excavations at the Late Bronze Age Mining Settlement at Apliki Karamallos, Cyprus*. Studies in Mediterranean Archaeology 134.1. Sävedalen, Sweden: P. Åström's Förlag.

Knapp, A.B., 1973. Mycenaean Pottery at Ugarit: Some Historical and Chronological Reflections. Unpublished MA thesis, University of California, Berkeley.

Knapp, A.B., 1983. An Alashiyan merchant at Ugarit. *Tel Aviv* 10: 38–45.

Knapp, A.B., 1991. Spice, drugs, grain and grog: organic goods in Bronze Age eastern Mediterranean trade. In N.H. Gale (ed.), *Bronze Age Trade in the Mediterranean*. Studies in Mediterranean Archaeology 90: 21–68. Göteborg: P. Åström's Förlag.

Knapp, A.B., 1993. Thalassocracies in Bronze Age eastern Mediterranean trade: making and breaking a myth. *World Archaeology* 24: 332–347.

Knapp, A.B., 1994. Emergence, development and decline on Bronze Age Cyprus. In C. Mathers and S. Stoddart (eds), *Development and Decline in the Mediterranean Bronze Age*. Sheffield Archaeological Monograph 8: 271–304. Sheffield: John Collis Publications.

Knapp, A.B., 1996a. The Bronze Age economy of Cyprus: ritual, ideology and the sacred landscape. In V. Karageorghis and D. Michaelides (eds), *The Development of the Cypriot Economy*, 71–106. Nicosia: University of Cyprus and the Bank of Cyprus.

Knapp, A.B., 1996b (ed.). *Near Eastern and Aegean Texts from the Third to the First Millennia BC*. Sources for the History of Cyprus II (edited by P.W. Wallace and A.G. Orphanides). Altamont, New York: Greece/Cyprus Research Center.

Knapp, A.B., 1998. Mediterranean Bronze Age trade: distance, power and place. In E.H. Cline and D. Harris-Cline (eds), *The Aegean and the Orient in the Second Millennium*. Aegaeum 18: 260–280. Liège: Université de Liège.

Knapp, A.B., 2006. Orientalisation and prehistoric Cyprus: the social life of Oriental goods. In C. Riva and N. Vella (eds), *Debating Orientalization: Multidisciplinary Approaches to Change in the Ancient Mediterranean*. Monographs in Mediterranean Archaeology 10: 48–65. London: Equinox Press.

Knapp, A.B., 2008. *Prehistoric and Protohistoric Cyprus: Identity, Insularity and Connectivity*. Oxford: Oxford University Press.

Knapp, A.B., 2012. Metallurgical production and trade on Bronze Age Cyprus: views and variations. In V. Kassianidou and G. Papasavvas (eds), *Eastern Mediterranean Metallurgy and Metalwork in the Second Millennium BC*, 14–25. Oxford: Oxbow.

Knapp, A.B., 2013. *The Archaeology of Cyprus: From Earliest Prehistory through the Bronze Age*. Cambridge: Cambridge University Press.

Knapp, A.B., 2018. *Seafaring and Seafarers in the Bronze Age Eastern Mediterranean*. Leiden: Sidestone Press.

Knapp, A.B., 2022. Bronze Age Cyprus and the Aegean: 'exotic currency' and objects of connectivity. *Journal of Greek Archaeology* 7: 67–93.

Knapp, A.B., and J.F. Cherry, 1994. *Provenience Studies and Bronze Age Cyprus: Production, Exchange, and Politico-Economic Change*. Monographs in World Archaeology 21. Madison, Wisconsin: Prehistory Press.

Knapp, A.B., and S. Demesticha, 2017. *Mediterranean Connections: Maritime Transport Containers and Seaborne Trade in the Bronze and Early Iron Ages*. London, New York: Routledge.

Knapp, A.B., and V. Kassianidou, 2008. The archaeology of Late Bronze Age copper production: Politiko *Phorades* on Cyprus. In Ü. Yalçin (ed.), *Anatolian Metal IV: Frühe Rohstoffgewinnung in Anatolien und seinen Nachbarländern*. Die Anschnitt, Beiheft 21. Veröffentlichungen aus dem Deutschen Bergbau-Museum 157: 135–147. Bochum: Deutsches Bergbau-Museum.

Knapp, A.B., and N. Meyer, 2023. Merchants and mercantile society on Late Bronze Age Cyprus. *American Journal of Archaeology* 127: 309–338.

Knapp, A.B., A. Russell and P. van Dommelen, 2022. Cyprus, Sardinia and Sicily: a maritime perspective on interaction, connectivity and imagination in Mediterranean prehistory. *Cambridge Archaeological Journal* 32: 79–97.

Knappett, C., 2000. The provenance of Red Lustrous wheel-made ware: Cyprus, Syria, or Anatolia? *Internet Archaeology* 9. DOI:10.11141/ia.9.7.

Knappett, C., and V. Kilikoglou, 2007. Provenancing Red Lustrous Wheelmade Ware: scales of analysis and floating fabrics. In I. Hein (ed.), *The Lustrous Wares of Late Bronze Age Cyprus and the Eastern Mediterranean*. Contributions to the Chronology of the Eastern Mediterranean 13: 115–140. Vienna: Österreichische Akademie der Wissenschaften.

Kopytoff, I., 1986. The cultural biography of things: commoditization as process. In A. Appadurai (ed.), *The Social Life of Things: Commodities in Cultural Perspective*, 64–91. Cambridge: Cambridge University Press.

Kostopoulou, I., 2024. Eastern Mediterranean exchange networks: imported ceramics at Pyla *Kokkinokremos*, Cyprus. In T. Bürge and L. Recht (eds), *Dynamics and Developments of Social Structures and Networks in Prehistoric and Protohistoric Cyprus*, 218–235. London, New York: Routledge.

Kozal, E., S. Hacıosmanoğlu, M. Kibaroğlu and G. Sunal, 2020. General outlook on the connections between Alalakh and Cyprus in the Middle and Late Bronze Ages: textual, archaeological and archaeometric studies. In K.A. Yener and T. Ingman (eds), *Alalakh and its Neighbours*. Ancient Near Eastern Studies, Supplement 55: 419–432. Leuven: Peeters.

Lackenbacher, S., and F. Malbran-Labat, 2016. *Lettres en akkadien de la 'Maison d'Urtenu'. Fouilles de 1994*. Ras Shamra-Ougarit 23. Louvain: Peeters.

Lagarce, J., 1993. Enkomi, fouilles françaises. In M. Yon (ed.), *Kinyras: L'archéologie française à Chypre*. Masion de l'Orient, Travaux 22: 91–106. Lyon: Masion de l'Orient.

Lagarce, J., and E. Lagarce. 1985. *Alasia IV. Deux Tombes du Chypriote Récent d'Enkomi. Tombes 1851 et 1907*. Mission Archéologique d'Alasia 7. Recherches sur les Civilisations, Memoire 51. Paris: ADPF.

Lagarce, J., and E. Lagarce, 1986. Les découvertes d'Enkomi et leur place dans la culture internationale du bronze récent. In J.-C. Courtois, J. Lagarce and E. Lagarce, *Enkomi et le Bronze Récent en Chypre*, 59–199. Nicosia: Leventis Foundation.

Lagarce, J., and E. Lagarce, 1995. Ras ibn-Hani au Bronze Récent: recherches et réflexions en cours. In M. Yon, M. Sznycer and P. Bordreuil (eds), *Le pays d'Ougarit autour de 1200 av. J.-C.* Ras Shamra-Ougarit 11: 141–154. Paris: Éditions Recherche sur les Civilisations.

Lagarce, J., and E. Lagarce, 1997. Les lingots 'en peau de boeuf'. Objets de commerce et symboles idélogues dans le monde Méditerranéen. *Revue des Études Phéniciennes-Puniques* 10: 73–79.

Lagarce, J., E. Lagarce, E. Bounni and N. Saliby, 1983. Les fouilles à Ras Ibn Hani en Syrie (campagnes de 1980, 1981 et 1982): contribution à l'étude de quelques aspects de la civilisation ugaritique. *Academie des Inscriptions et Belles-Lettres: Comptes Rendus des Séances*: 249–290.

Lamaze, J., 2022. Games and oracular practices around the hearth: the 'table of offerings' from the so-called Temple 4 at Kition *Kathari* (Cyprus). *Board Game Studies* 16: 95–128. DOI:10.2478/bgs-2022-0004.

Laroche, E., 1968. Documents en Hourrite alphabétique de Ras Shamra. In C.F.A. Schaeffer (ed.), *Ugaritica* 5. Mission de Ras Shamra 16: 447–544. Paris: Geuthner.

Leidwanger, J., and C. Knappett (eds), 2018. *Maritime Networks in the Ancient Mediterranean World*. Cambridge: Cambridge University Press.

Linder, E., 1981. Ugarit: a Canaanite thalassocracy. In G.D. Young (ed.), *Ugarit in Retrospect*, 31–42. Winona Lake, Indiana: Eisenbrauns.

Linkov, I., S.E. Galaitsi, B.D. Trump, E. Pinigina, K. Rand, E.H. Cline and M. Kitsak, 2024. Are civilizations destined to collapse? Lessons from the Mediterranean Bronze Age. *Global Environmental Change* 84: 102792. DOI:10.1016/j.gloenvcha.2023.102792.

Liverani, M., 1962. *Storia du Ugarit*. Studi Semitici 6. Rome: Università di Roma.

Liverani, M., 1983. Political lexicon and political ideologies in the Amarna letters. *Berytus* 31: 41–56.

Liverani, M., 1990. *Prestige and Interest: International Relations in the Near East ca. 1600-1100 BC*. Padova: Sargon Press.

Macke, S., A. Yasur-Landau, E. Galili, G. Yasur, T. Zilberman and R. Shahack-Gross, 2023. Provenance of Bronze Age stone anchors, a case study from the Carmel coast, Israel. *Journal of Archaeological Science, Reports* 48: 103891. DOI:10.1016/j.jasrep.2023.103891.

Maguire, L.C., 2009. *The Cypriot Pottery and its Circulation in the Levant.* Tell el-Dab'a 21. Österreichische Akademie der Wissenschaften, Denkschriften der Gesamtakademie 51. Vienna: Österreichische Akademie der Wissenschaften,

Maier, F.-G., and V. Karageorghis, 1984. *Paphos: History and Archaeology.* Nicosia: Leventis Foundation.

Malbran-Labat, F., 1999. Nouvelles données épigraphiques sur Chypre et Ougarit. *Report of the Department of Antiquities, Cyprus*: 121–123.

Manning, S.W., and F.A. DeMita, Jr., 1997. Cyprus, the Aegean and Maroni *Tsaroukkas*. In D. Christou (ed.), *Cyprus and the Aegean in Antiquity*, 103–142. Nicosia: Department of Antiquities, Cyprus.

Manning, S.W., D. Sewell and E. Herscher, 2001. Late Cypriot IA maritime trade in action: underwater survey at Maroni *Tsaroukkas* and the contemporary east Mediterranean trading system. *Annual of the British School at Athens* 97: 97–162.

Manning, S.W., L. Crewe and D.A. Sewell, 2006. Further light on early LC I connections at Maroni. In E. Czerny, I. Hein, H. Hunger, D. Melman and A. Schwab (eds), *Timelines. Studies in Honour of Manfred Bietak* 2. Orientalia Lovaniensia Analecta 149(2): 471–488. Leuven: Uitgeverij Peeters en Departement Oosterse Studies.

Marchegay, S., 1999. Les tombes d'Ougarit: architecture, localisation et relation avec l'habitat. Unpublished PhD thesis, Université Lyon-2.

Marchegay, S., 2000. The tombs. *Near Eastern Archaeology* 63: 208–209.

Marchegay, S., 2001. Un plan des fouilles 1929-1935 à Minet el-Beida, le port d'Ougarit. In M. Yon and D. Arnaud (eds), *Études Ougaritiques* I. *Travaux 1985-1995*. Ras Shamra-Ougarit 14: 11–40. Paris: Éditions Recherche sur les Civilisations.

Marchegay, S., 2008. Les pratiques funéraires à Ougarit au IIe millénaire: bilan et perspectives des recherches. In Y. Calvet and M. Yon (eds.), *Ras Shamra-Ougarit au Bronze Moyen et au Bronze Récent.* Travaux de la Maison de l'Orient et la Méditeranée 47: 97–118. Lyon: Maison de l'Orient et la Méditeranée.

Margueron, J., 1977. Ras Shamra 1975 et 1976. Rapport préliminaire sur les campagnes d'automne. *Syria* 54: 151–188.

Margueron, J.-C., 2008. Ugarit: gateway to the Mediterranean. In J. Aruz, K. Benzel and J.M. Evans (eds), *Beyond Babylon: Art, Trade, and Diplomacy in the Second Millennium BC*, 236–238. New York: Metropolitan Museum of Art.

Masson, E., 1974. *Cyprominoica. Repertoires Documents de Ras Shamra. Essais d'Interpretation*. Studies in Mediterranean Archaeology 31.2. Göteborg: P. Åström's Förlag.

Masson, E., 1976. À la recherche des vestiges proche-orientaux à Chypre, fin du bronze moyen et début du bronze récent. *Archäologischer Anzeiger* (1976:2): 139–165.

Masson, E., 1983. Premiers documents Chypro-Minoens du site Kalavasos *Ayios Dhimitrios*. *Report of the Department of Antiquities, Cyprus*: 131–141.

Masson, O., 1956. Documents chypro-minoens trouvé à Enkomi. In C.F. A. Schaeffer, *Ugaritica* III. Mission de Ras Shamra 7, Bibliothèque Archéologique et Historique 64: 233–250. Paris: Geuthner.

Masson, O., 1969. Documents chypro-minoens de Ras Shamra III. La tablette RS 20.25 de 1956. In C.F.A. Schaeffer (ed.), *Ugaritica* 6. Mission de Ras Shamra 17, Bibliothèque Archéologique et Historique 81: 379–392. Paris: Geuthner.

Matoïan, V. (ed.), 2017. *Archéologie, patrimoine et archives: les fouilles anciennes à Ras Shamra et à Minet el-Beida* I. Ras Shamra-Ougarit 25. Louvain: Peeters.

Matoïan, V., 2018. Nouvelles données sur les monuments de l'Acropole de Ras Shamra-Ougarit (Syrie). *Academie des Inscriptions et Belles-Lettres: Comptes Rendus des Séances* (2018.1): 253–305.

Matoïan, V. (ed.), 2019. *Archéologie, patrimoine et archives: les fouilles anciennes à Ras Shamra et à Minet el-Beida* II. Ras Shamra-Ougarit 26. Louvain: Peeters.

Matoïan, V. (ed.), 2021a. *Ougarit, un anniveraire: bilans et recherches en cours*. Ras Shamra-Ougarit 28. Louvain: Peeters.

Matoïan, V., 2021b. Une correspondance entre Vere Gordon Childe et Claude Schaeffer, l'année 1948. *Semitica* 63: 5–28.

Matoïan, V., 2021c. Représentations de bateaux à Ugarit: réexamen du document RS19.199 découvert dans le 'Palais Sud'/'maison de Yabninu'. *Ugarit-Forschungen* 52: 127–148.

Matoïan, V., and A. Carbillet, 2017. Baignoires en pierre de Ras Shamra–Ougarit. In V. Matoïan (ed.), *Archéologie, patrimoine et archives: les fouilles anciennes à Ras Shamra et à Minet el-Beida* I. Ras Shamra-Ougarit 25: 209–240. Louvain: Peeters.

Matoïan, V., and J.-P. Vita, 2018. The administration of wine in Ugarit. *Die Welt des Orients* 48: 299–318.

Matoïan, V., and J.-P. Vita, 2020. Proportional weights of metals in Ugarit. *Semitica* 62: 21–42.

Mazar, A., 1988. A note on Canaanite jars from Enkomi. *Israel Exploration Journal* 38: 224–226.

Mazow, L.B., 2014. The root of the problem: on the relationship between wool processing and lanolin production. *Journal of Mediterranean Archaeology* 27: 33–50.

McCaslin, D., 1980. *Stone Anchors in Antiquity: Coastal Settlements and Maritime Trade-Routes in the Eastern Mediterranean ca.1600-1050 B.C*. Studies in Mediterranean Archaeology 61. Göteborg: P. Åström's Förlag.

McGeough, K.M., 2015. 'What is not in my house you must give me': agents of exchange according to the textual evidence from Ugarit. In B. Eder and R. Pruzsinszky (eds), *Policies of Exchange: Political Systems and Modes of Interaction in the Aegean and the Near East in the 2nd Millennium B.C.E.* Oriental and European Archaeology 2: 85–96. Vienna: Österreichische Akademie der Wissenschaften.

Meneghetti, F., 2022-23. Cyprus™: looking for branding practices in Late Bronze Age Cyprus. *Cahiers du Centre d'Études Chypriotes* 52-53: 93–116.

Merrillees, R.S., 1974. *Trade and Transcendance in the Bronze Age Levant*. Studies in Mediterranean Archaeology 39. Göteborg: P. Åström's Förlag.

Merrillees, R.S., 1978. El-Lisht and Tell el-Yahudiyeh ware in the Archaeological Museum of the American University of Beirut. *Levant* 10: 75–98.

Merrillees, R.S., 2007. The ethnic implications of Tell el-Yahudiyeh ware for the history of the Middle to Late Bronze Age in Cyprus. *Cahier du Centre d'Études Chypriotes* 37: 87–96.

Meyer, N., 2024. Continuity within discontinuity: Cypriot political forms from the Late Bronze Age to the Early Iron Age. *European Journal of Archaeology.* DOI:10.1017/eaa.2024.25.

Meyer, N., and A.B. Knapp, 2021. Resilient social actors in the transition from the Late Bronze to the Early Iron Age on Cyprus. *Journal of World Prehistory* 34: 433–487.

Miller, A., Y. Me-Bar and D. Cvikel, 2023. Judging a ship by its anchor: Bronze Age stone weight anchors as indicators of ship size. *Journal of Archaeological Science, Reports* 52: 104284. DOI:10.1016/j.jasrep.2023.104284.

Monchambert, J.-Y., 1983. Céramique de fabrication local à Ougarit à la fin du Bronze Récent: quelques exemples. *Syria* 60: 25–45.

Monchambert, J.-Y., 2004. *La céramique d'Ougarit. Campagnes de fouilles 1975 et 1976.* Ras Shamra-Ougarit 15. Paris: Éditions Recherche sur les Civilisations.

Monroe, C., 2009. *Scales of Fate: Trade, Tradition, and Transformation in the Eastern Mediterranean.* Alter Orient und Altes Testament 357. Münster: Ugarit-Verlag.

Monroe, C., 2011. 'From luxuries to anxieties': a liminal view of the Late Bronze Age world-system. In T.C. Wilkinson, S. Sherratt and J. Bennett (eds), *Interweaving Worlds: Systemic Interactions in Eurasia, 7th to the 1st Millennia BC*, 87–99. Oxford: Oxbow.

Monroe, C., 2015. Tangled up in blue: material and other relations of exchange in the Late Bronze Age world. In T. Howe (ed.), *Traders in the Ancient Mediterranean.* Publications of the Association of Ancient Historians 11: 7–46. Chicago: Ares Publishers.

Monroe, C., 2016. Measure for 'measure': connecting text to material culture through Late Bronze Age shipping jars. In S. Demesticha and A.B. Knapp (eds), *Maritime Transport Containers in the Bronze–Iron Age Aegean and Eastern Mediterranean.* Studies in Mediterranean Archaeology and Literature PB 183: 79–96. Uppsala: Åströms Förlag.

Monroe, C., 2022. All the king's wine? Late Bronze Age vineyards in texts from Emar and Ugarit. In S.W. Manning (ed.), *Critical Approaches to Cypriot and Wider Mediterranean Archaeology.* Monographs in Mediterranean Archaeology 16: 217–233. Sheffield: Equinox.

Mountjoy, P.A., and H. Mommsen, 2015. Neutron Activation Analysis of Aegean-style IIIC pottery from 11 Cypriot and various Near Eastern sites. *Ägypten und Levante* 25: 421–508.

Muhly, J.D., R. Maddin and T. Stech, 1988. Cyprus, Crete and Sardinia: copper oxhide ingots and the metals trade. *Report of the Department of Antiquities, Cyprus*: 281–298.

Muniz A., and T.C. O'Guinn, 2001. Brand communities. *Journal of Consumer Research* 27: 412–432.

Murray, A.S., A.H. Smith and H.B. Walters, 1900. *Excavations in Cyprus.* London: British Museum Publications.

Murray, S.C., 2023a. *Long-distance Exchange and Inter-regional Economies.* Elements in the Aegean Bronze Age. Cambridge: Cambridge University Press.

Murray, S.C., 2023b. Eastern Mediterranean Bronze Age trade in archaeological perspective: a review of interpretative and empirical developments. *Journal of Archaeological Research* 31: 395–447.

Negbi, O., 1978. Cypriote imitations of Tell el-Yahudiyeh ware from Toumba tou Skourou. *American Journal of Archaeology* 82: 137–149.

Nigro, L., 2003. The smith and the king of Ebla: Tell el-Yahudiyeh Ware, Metallic Wares and the ceramic chronology of Middle Bronze Syria. In M. Bietak (ed.), *The Synchronisation of Civilisations in the Eastern Mediterranean in the Second Millennium BC* II. Denkschrfiten der Gesamtakademie 29, Contributions to the Chronology of the Eastern Mediterranean 4: 345–363. Vienna: Österreichischen Akademie der Wissenschaften.

Nougayrol, J., 1955. *Le Palais Royal d'Ugarit* 3. Mission de Ras Shamra 6. Paris: Klincksieck.

Nougayrol, J., 1956. *Palais Royal d'Ugarit* 4. Mission de Ras Shamra 9. Paris: Klincksieck.

Nougayrol, J., E. Laroche, C. Virolleaud and C.F.A. Schaeffer, 1968. *Ugaritica* 5. Mission de Ras Shamra 16. Paris: Geuthner.

Oka, R., and C.M. Kusimba, 2008. The archaeology of trading systems, part 1: towards a new trade synthesis. *Journal of Archaeological Research* 16: 339–395.

Overbeck, J.C., and S. Swiny, 1972. *Two Cypriot Bronze Age Sites at Kafkallia (Dhali)*. Studies in Mediterranean Archaeology 33. Göteborg: P. Åström's Förlag.

Ownby, M., and M.V. Smith, 2011. The impact of changing political situations on trade between Egypt and the Near East: a provenance study of Canaanite jars from Memphis, Egypt. In K. Duistermaat and I. Regulski (eds), *Intercultural Contacts in the Ancient Mediterranean*. Orientalia Lovaniensia Analecta 202: 267–284. Louvain: Peeters.

Palaima, T.G., 1989. Cypro-Minoan scripts: problems of historical context. In Y. Duhoux, T.G. Palaima and J. Bennet (eds), *Problems in Decipherment*, 121–187. Louvain: Peeters.

Palaima, T.G., 2005. *The Triple Invention of Writing in Cyprus and Written Sources for Cypriote History*. Nicosia: Leventis Foundation, Leventis Municipal Museum.

Panagiotopoulos, D., 2011. The stirring sea: conceptualising transculturality in the Late Bronze Age eastern Mediterranean. In K. Duistermaat and I. Regulski (eds), *Intercultural Contacts in the Ancient Mediterranean*. Orientalia Lovaniensia Analecta 202: 31–51. Louvain: Peeters.

Panagiotopoulos, D., 2012. Encountering the foreign. (De-)constructing alterity in the archaeologies of the Bronze Age Mediterranean. In J. Maran and P. Stockhammer (eds), *Materiality and Social Practice: Transformative Capacities of Intercultural Encounters*, 51–60. Oxford: Oxbow.

Papadimitriou, N., 2013. Regional or 'international' networks? A comparative examination of Aegean and Cypriot imported pottery in the eastern Mediterranean. In A. Papadopoulos (ed.), *Recent Research and Perspectives on the Late Bronze Age Eastern Mediterranean*. Talanta 44: 92–136. Amsterdam: Dutch Historical and Archaeological Society.

Papasavvas, G., 2003. Cypriot casting technology I: the stands. *Report of the Department of Antiquities, Cyprus*: 23–52.

Papasavvas, G., 2012. Profusion of Cypriot copper abroad, dearth of bronzes at home: a paradox in Late Bronze Age Cyprus. In V. Kassianidou and G. Papasavvas (eds), *Eastern Mediterranean Metallurgy and Metalwork in the Second Millennium BC*, 117–128. Oxford: Oxbow.

Papasavvas, G., 2018. Values, weights and equivalences of metals in the Late Bronze Age eastern Mediterranean, or what could a copper oxhide ingot 'buy'? In A. Giumlia-Mair and F. Lo Schiavo (eds), *Bronze Age Metallurgy in the Mediterranean Islands. In Honour of Robert Maddin and Vassos Karageorghis*. Monographies Instrumentum 56: 600–629. Auteuil, France: Éditions Mergoil.

Papasavvas, G., 2021. What could a copper oxhide ingot 'buy' in the markets of the Late Bronze Age eastern Mediterranean? In M. Perra and F. Lo Schiavo (eds), *Cultural Contacts and Trade in Nuragic Sardinia: The Southern Route (Sardinia, Sicily, Crete and Cyprus)*, 127–150. Cagliari: Arkadia Editore.

Papasavvas, G., 2023. *Trench Warfare at Enkomi: Personalities, Politics and Science in Cypriot Archaeology*. Studies in Mediterranean Archaeology and Literature, PB 193. Nicosia: Astrom Editions.

Pardee, D. 2012. RS 18.113A+B, lettre d'un serviteur du roi d'Ougarit se trouvant à Chypre. In G.A. Kiraz and Z. Al-Salameen (eds.), *From Ugarit to Nabataea, Studies in Honor of John F. Healey*. Gorgias Ugaritic Studies 6: 167–206. Piscataway, New Jersey: Gorgias Press.

Pardee, D., 2023. The "merchants" of Ugarit: the textual evidence. *Semitica et Classica* 16: 41–104.

Parr, P.J., 1973. The origin of the Canaanite jar. In D.E. Strong (ed.), *Archaeological Theory and Practice: Festschrift W.F. Grimes*, 173–181. London, New York: Seminar Press.

Pearlman, D., 1985. Kalavassos village, tomb 51: tomb of an unknown soldier. *Report of the Department of Antiquities, Cyprus*: 164–179.

Pedrazzi, T., 2016. Canaanite jars and the maritime trade network in the northern Levant during the transition from the Late Bronze to the early Iron Age. In S. Demesticha and A.B. Knapp (eds), *Maritime Transport Containers in the Bronze–Iron Age Aegean and Eastern Mediterranean*. Studies in Mediterranean Archaeology and Literature, PB 183: 57–77. Uppsala: Åströms Förlag.

Pedrazzi, T., 2022. Canaanite jars in Cyprus in the 13th–12th centuries BC. Transfer of goods, transformation of networks. In G. Bourogiannis (ed.), *Beyond Cyprus: Investigating Cypriot Connectivity in the Mediterranean from the Late Bronze Age to the End of the Classical Period*. AURA Supplement 9: 119–130. Athens: Faculty of History and Archaeology, University of Athens.

Peltenburg, E., 1974. The glazed vases (including a polychrome rhyton). Appendix I. In V. Karageorghis, *Excavations at Kition* I. *The Tombs*, 105–144. Nicosia: Department of Antiquities, Cyprus.

Peltenburg, E., 1995. Kissonerga in Cyprus and the appearance of faience in the east Mediterranean. In S. Bourke and J.-P. Descoeudres (eds), *Trade, Contact, and the Movement of People in the Eastern Mediterranean*. Mediterranean Archaeology, Supplement 3: 31–41. Sydney: Department of Archaeology, University of Sydney.

Peltenburg, E., 2002. East Mediterranean faience: changing patterns of production and exchange at the end of the 2nd millennium BC. In E.A. Braun-Holzinger and H. Matthäus (eds), *Die nahöstlichen Kulturen und Griechenland an der Wende zum 2 zum 1 Jahrtausend v. Chr.*, 75–107. Möhnesee: Bibliopolis.

Peltenburg, E., 2007. Hathor, faience and copper on Late Bronze Age Cyprus. *Cahier du Centre d'Études Chypriotes* 37: 375–394.

Peltenburg, E.J., 2012. King Kushmeshusha and the decentralised political structure of Late Bronze Age Cyprus. In G. Cadogan, M. Iacovou, K. Kopaka and J. Whitley (eds), *Parallel Lives: Ancient Island Societies in Crete and Cyprus*. British School at Athens, Studies 20: 345–351. London: British School at Athens.

Philip, G., 1991. Cypriot bronzework in the Levantine world: conservatism, innovation and social change. *Journal of Mediterranean Archaeology* 4: 59–107.

Philokyprou, M., 2011. The initial appearance of ashlar stone in Cyprus: issues of provenance and use. *Mediterranean Archaeology and Archaeometry* 11: 37–53.

Pickles, S., and E.J. Peltenburg, 1998. Metallurgy, society and the Bronze/Iron transition in the east Mediterranean and the Near East. *Report of the Department of Antiquities, Cyprus*: 67–100.

Pieniazek, M., P. Pavúk and E. Kozal, 2018. The Troad, south Aegean, and the eastern Mediterranean: long-distance connections during the Middle and Late Bronze Age. In B. Nessel, D. Neumann and M. Bertelheim (eds), *Bronzezeitlicher Transport: Akteure, Mittel und Wege*. Resourcen Kulturen 8: 375–410. Tübingen: Tübingen University Press.

Porta, F., and V. Cannavò, 2024. Pyla *Kokkinokremos* (Cyprus) and Late Bronze Age Mediterranean networks: the role of the pithoi. In T. Bürge and L. Recht (eds), *Dynamics and Developments of Social Structures and Networks in Prehistoric and Protohistoric Cyprus*, 236–254. London, New York: Routledge.

Pulak, C., 2008. The Uluburun shipwreck and Late Bronze Age trade. In J. Aruz, K. Benzel and J.M. Evans (eds.), *Beyond Babylon: Art, Trade, and Diplomacy in the Second Millennium BC*, 289–310. New York, New Haven and London: Metropolitan Museum of Art, Yale University Press.

Reese, D.S., 2018. Invertebrates. In P.M. Fischer and T. Bürge, *Two Late Cypriot City Quarters at Hala Sultan Tekke. The Söderberg Expedition 2010–2017*. Studies in Mediterranean Archaeology 147: 532–563. Uppsala: Åström Editions.

Renson, V., D. Ben-Shlomo, J. Coenaerts, K. Charbit-Nataf, M. Samaes, N. Mattielli, K. Nys and Ph. Claeys, 2013. Using lead isotopes to determine pottery provenance in Cyprus: clay source signatures and comparison with Late Bronze Age Cypriote pottery. *Geoarchaeology* 28: 517–530.

Renson, V., D. Ben-Shlomo, J. Coenaerts, K. Charbit-Nataf, M. Samaes, N. Mattielli, K. Nys and Ph. Claeys, 2014. Coupling lead isotope analysis and petrography to characterize fabrics of storage and trade containers from Hala Sultan Tekke (Cyprus). *Archaeometry* 56: 261–278.

Richey, M., 2023. Syria, Mesopotamia and the origins of the alphabet. *Maarav* 27: 1–38.

Riehle, K., E. Kistler, B. Öhlinger … R. Posamentir and U. Schlotzhauer, 2023. Neutron activation analysis in Mediterranean archaeology: current applications and future perspectives. *Archaeological and Anthropological Sciences* 15:25. DOI:10.1007/s12520-023-01728-1.

Roche-Hawley, C., 2023. A synthetic view of the House of Urtenu at Ugarit and its contribution to our understanding of the end of the Late Bronze Age in the eastern Mediterranean. In T. Bürge and P.M. Fischer (eds), *The Decline of Bronze Age Civilisations in the Mediterranean: Cyprus and Beyond*. Studies in Mediterranean Archaeology 154: 39–49. Nicosia: Åstrom Editions.

Saade, G., 1995. Le port d'Ougarit. In M. Yon, M. Sznycer and P. Bordreuil (eds), *Le pays d'Ougarit autour de 1200 av. J.-C.* Ras Shamra-Ougarit 11: 211–225. Paris: Éditions Recherche sur les Civilisations.

Safadi, C., 2016. Wind and wave modelling for the evaluation of the maritime accessibility and protection afforded by ancient harbours. *Journal of Archaeological Science, Reports* 5: 348–360.

Salles, J.-F., 1987. Deux nouvelles tombes de Ras Shamra. In M. Yon, *Le Centre de la Ville, 38e-44e Campagne (1978-1984)*. Ras Shamra-Ougarit 3. Éditions Recherches sur les Civilisations, Memoire 72: 157–195. Paris: ADPF.

Salles, J.-F., 1995. Rituel mortuaire et rituel social à Ras Shamra/Ougarit. In S. Campbell and A. Green (eds), *The Archaeology of Death in the Ancient Near East*. Oxbow Monograph 51: 171–184. Oxford: Oxbow Books.

Sass, B., 2017. The emergence of monumental West Semitic alphabetic writing, with an emphasis on Byblos. *Semitica* 59: 109–141.

Sauvage, C., 2006. Warehouses and the economic system of the city of Ugarit. The example of the 80-jar deposit and deposit 213 from Minet el-Beida. *Ugarit-Forschungen* 38: 617–629.

Sauvage, C., 2012. *Routes maritimes et systèmes d'échanges internationaux au Bronze récent en Méditerranée orientale*. Travaux de la Maison de l'Orient et de la Méditerranée 61. Lyon: Maison de l'Orient et de la Méditerranée–Jean Pouilloux.

Sauvage, C., 2015. Nouvelle réflexion sur le dépôt aux 80 jarres de Minet el-Beida. In B. Geyer, V. Matoïan and M. Al-Maqdissi (eds), *De l'île d'Aphrodite au Paradis perdu, itinéraire d'un gentilhomme lyonnais, en hommage à Yves Calvet*. Ras Shamra-Ougarit 22: 63–76. Leuven: Peeters.

Sauvage, C., 2022. Note on a White Lustrous Wheel-made ware spindle bottle from Ras Shamra. *Bulletin of ASOR* 388: 133–152.

Sauvage, C., 2024. The materiality of textiles and textile tools in the Late Bronze Age eastern Mediterranean. *Archaeological Textiles Review* 65: 30–48.

Sauvage, C., and C. Lorre, 2023. *À la découverte du royaume d'Ougarit (Syrie du IIe millénaire). Les fouilles de C.F.A. Schaeffer à Minet el-Beida et Ras Shamra (1929-1937)*. Contributions to the Archaeology of Egypt, Nubia and the Levant 7, Denkschriften der Gesamtakademie 89. Vienna: Österreichischen Akademie der Wissenschaften.

Schaeffer, C.F.A., 1931. Les fouilles de Minet el-Beidha et de Ras Shamra, deuxième campagne (printemps 1930). *Syria* 12: 1–14.

Schaeffer, C.F.A., 1932. Les fouilles de Minet el-Beidha et de Ras Shamra, troisième campagne (printemps 1931). *Syria* 13: 1–27.

Schaeffer, C.F.A., 1933. Les fouilles de Minet el-Beidha et de Ras Shamra. *Syria* 14: 93–127.

Schaeffer, C.F.A., 1935. Las fouilles de Ras-Shamra: sixième campagne (printemps 1934), rapport sommaire. *Syria* 16: 141–176.

Schaeffer, C.F.A., 1936a. *Missions en Chypre, 1932-1935*. Paris: Geuthner.

Schaeffer, C.F.A., 1936b. Fouilles de Ras Shamra-Ugarit: septième campagne (printemps 1935). *Syria* 17: 105–149.

Schaeffer, C.F.A., 1939. *Ugaritica* I. Mission de Ras Shamra 3, Bibliothèque Archéologique et Historique 31. Paris: Geuthner.

Schaeffer, C.F.A., 1948. *Stratigraphie comparée et Chronologie de l'Asie Occidentale (IIIe et IIe millénaires), Syrie, Palestine, Asie Mineure, Chypre, Perse et Caucase*. Oxford, London: Griffith Institute, Ashmolean Museum, Oxford University Press.

Schaeffer, C.F.A., 1949. *Ugaritica* II. Mission de Ras Shamra 5, Bibliothèque Archéologique et Historique 47. Paris: Geuthner.

Schaeffer, C.F.A., 1952. *Enkomi-Alasia* I. *Nouvelles Missions en Chypre 1946-1950*. Paris: Klincksieck.

Schaeffer, C.F.A., 1968. Commentaires sur les lettres et documents trouvées dans les bibliothèques privées d'Ugarit. In J. Nougayrol, E. Laroche, C. Virolleaud and C.F.A. Schaeffer, *Ugaritica* 5. Mission de Ras Shamra 16: 607–768. Paris: Geuthner.

Schaeffer, C.F.A., 1971. *Alasia* I. Mission Archéologique d'Alasia 4. Paris: Klincksieck.

Schaeffer, C.F.A. (ed.), 1978. *Ugaritica* 7. Mission de Ras Shamra 18, Bibliothèque Archéologique et Historique 99. Paris: Geuthner.

Schaeffer, C.F.A., 1983. *Corpus des cylindres-sceaux de Ras Shamra-Ugarit et d'Enkomi-Alasia*. Paris: Éditions Recherches sur les Civilisations.

Schloen, J. D., 2001. *The House of the Father as Fact and Symbol: Patrimonalism in Ugarit and the Ancient Near East*. Studies in the Archaeology and History of the Levant 2. Winona Lake, Indiana: Eisenbrauns.

Serpico, M., J. Bourriau, L. Smith, Y. Goren, B. Stern and C. Heron, 2003. Commodities and containers: a project to study Canaanite amphorae imported into Egypt during the New Kingdom. In M. Bietak (ed.), *The Synchronisation of Civilisations in the Eastern Mediterranean in the Second Millennium BC* II. Denkschrfiten der Gesamtakademie 29, Contributions to the Chronology of the Eastern Mediterranean 4: 365–375. Vienna: Österreichischen Akademie der Wissenschaften.

Shammas, S., 2023. *Tell el-Yahudiyeh Ware in the Northern Levant*. Münchener Abhandlungen zum Alten Orient 10. Gladbeck, Germany: PeWe-Verlag.

Shaw, J.W., 1995. Two three-holed stone anchors from Kommos, Crete: their context, type, and origin. *International Journal of Nautical Archaeology and Underwater Exploration* 24: 279–291.

Sherratt, A.G., and E.S. Sherratt, 1991. From luxuries to commodities: the nature of Mediterranean Bronze Age trading systems. In N.H. Gale (ed.), *Bronze Age Trade in the Mediterranean*. Studies in Mediterranean Archaeology 90: 351–386. Göteborg: P. Åström's Förlag.

Sherratt, E.S., 1991. Cypriot pottery of Aegean type in LCII-III: problems of classification, chronology and interpretation. In J. Barlow, D. Bolger, and B. Kling (eds), *Cypriot Ceramics: Reading the Prehistoric Record*. University Museum Monograph 74: 185–198. Philadelphia: University Museum, University of Pennsylvania.

Sherratt, E.S., 1998. 'Sea Peoples' and the economic structure of the late second millennium in the eastern Mediterranean. In S. Gitin, A. Mazar and E. Stern (eds), *Mediterranean Peoples in Transition: Thirteenth to Tenth Centuries BCE*, 292–313. Jerusalem: Israel Exploration Society.

Singer, I., 1999. A political history of Ugarit. In W.G.E. Watson and N. Wyatt (eds), *Handbook of Ugaritic Studies*. Handbuch der Orientalistik, Abteilung 1, Der Nahe und Mittlere Osten, Band 39: 603–733. Leiden: Brill.

Singer, I., 2006. Ships bound for Lukka: a new interpretation of the companion letters RS 94.2530 and RS 94.2523. *Altorientalische Forschungen* 33: 242–262.

Smith, J.S., 1994. Seals for Sealing in the Late Cypriot Period. Unpublished PhD dissertation, Bryn Mawr College, Bryn Mawr, Pennsylvania.

Smith, J.S., 2002. Problems and prospects in the study of script and seal use on Cyprus in the Bronze and Iron Ages. In J.S. Smith (ed.), *Script and Seal Use on Cyprus in the Bronze and Iron Ages*. AIA Colloquia and Conference Papers 4: 1–47. Boston: Archaeological Institute of America.

Smith, J.S., 2003. Writing styles in clay of the eastern Mediterranean Bronze Age. In N.C. Stampolidis and V. Karageorghis (eds), *Ploes.. Sea Routes...: Interconnections in the Mediterranean, 16th-6th c. BC*, 277–290. Athens: University of Crete, Leventis Foundation.

Smith, J.S., 2022. Cypriot seals and Cypriots overseas. In G. Bourogiannis (ed.), *Beyond Cyprus: Investigating Cypriot Connectivity in the Mediterranean from the Late Bronze Age to the End of the Classical Period*. AURA Supplement 9: 207–223. Athens: Faculty of History and Archaeology, University of Athens.

Smith, L.M.V., J. Bourriau, Y. Goren, M. J. Hughes and M. Serpico, 2004. The provenance of Canaanite amphorae found at Memphis and Amarna in the New Kingdom: results 2000-2002. In J. Bourriau and J. Phillips (eds), *Invention and Innovation: The Social Context of Technological Change 2: Egypt, the Aegean, and the Near East, 1650–1150 BC*, 55–77. Oxford: Oxbow.

Snape, S.R., 2003. Zawiyet Umm el-Rakham and Egyptian foreign trade in the 13th century BC. In N.C. Stampolidis and V. Karageorghis (eds), *Ploes.. Sea Routes...: Interconnections in the Mediterranean, 16th-6th c. BC*, 63–70. Athens: University of Crete, Leventis Foundation.

South, A.K., 1983. Kalavasos *Ayios Dhimitrios* 1982. *Report of the Department of Antiquities, Cyprus*: 92–116.

South, A.K., 1991. Kalavasos *Ayios Dhimitrios* 1990. *Report of the Department of Antiquities, Cyprus*: 131–139.

South, A.K., 1997. Kalavasos *Ayios Dhimitrios* 1992-1996. *Report of the Department of Antiquities, Cyprus*: 151–175.

South, A., 2008. Feasting in Cyprus: a view from Kalavasos. In L.A. Hitchcock, R. Laffineur and J. Crowley (eds), *DAIS. The Aegean Feast*. Aegaeum 29: 309–316. Liège, Austin: Université de Liège, University of Texas at Austin.

South, A.K., P. Russell and P.S. Keswani, 1989. *Kalavasos-Ayios Dhimitrios II (Ceramics, Objects, Tombs, Specialist Studies)*. Vasilikos Valley Project 3. Studies in Mediterranean Archaeology 71.3. Göteborg: P. Åström's Förlag.

Spathmann, K., 2021-22. Cypriot pottery. *Archaeology and History in the Lebanon* 54-55: 475–498.

Steel, L., 1998. The social impact of Mycenaean imported pottery on Cyprus. *Annual of the British School at Athens* 93: 285–296.

Steel, L., 2010. Late Cypriot ceramic production: heterarchy or hierarchy? In D. Bolger and L. Maguire (eds), *The Development of Pre-State Communities in the Ancient Near East. Studies in Honour of Edgar Peltenburg*. BANEA Publication Series 2: 106–116. Oxford: Oxbow.

Steel, L., 2013. *Materiality and Consumption in the Bronze Age Mediterranean*. Routledge Studies in Archaeology 7. London: Routledge.

Steel, L., 2016. Exploring Aredhiou: new light on the rural communities of the Cypriot hinterland during the Late Bronze Age. *American Journal of Archaeology* 120: 511–536.

Steel, L., 2022. Agencement, matter flows and itinerary of object in the Bronze Age east Mediterranean: a new materialities approach to globalization. In S. Autiero and M.A. Cobb (eds), *Globalization and Transculturality from Antiquity to the Pre-Modern World*, 81–102. London: Routledge.

Steel, L., 2023. Mycenaean pottery from the Cypriot hinterland: luxuries, commodities or oddities? In A.L. D'Agata and P. Pavúk (eds), *The Lady of Pottery: Ceramic Studies Presented to Penelope A. Mountjoy in Acknowledgement of Her Outstanding Scholarship*. Studi Micenei ed Egeo-Anatolici, n.s. Supplemento 3: 179–206. Rome: Edizioni Quasar.

Steel, L., and C. McCartney, 2008. Survey at Arediou *Vouppes* (*Lithosouros*), a Late Bronze Age agricultural settlement on Cyprus: a preliminary analysis of the material culture assemblages. *Bulletin of the American Schools of Oriental Research* 351: 9–37.

Steel, L., and S. Thomas, 2008. Excavations at Aredhiou *Vouppes* (*Lithosouros*): an interim report on excavations 2005-2006. *Report of the Department of Antiquities, Cyprus*: 227–249.

Steele, P.M., 2019. *Writing and Society in Ancient Cyprus*. Cambridge: Cambridge University Press.

Sürenhagen, D., 2001. Die Bezeichnung Zyperns (*Alasija*) zum hethitischen Reich und seinen nordsyrien Vassalen während der 2. Hälfte des 2. Jahrtausends v. Chr. In A. Kyriatsoulis (ed.), *Kreta und Zypern: Religion und Schrift. Von der Frühgeschichte biz zum Ende der archaischen Zeit*, 249–263. Altenburg: DZA Verlag für Kultur und Wissenschaft.

Susnow, M., C. McKinny and I. Shai, 2024. Object biographies, object agency and a local community's encounter with and response to foreign commodities: the pithoi from LB Tel Burna as a case study. *Cambridge Archaeological Journal*. DOI:10.1017/S0959774324000088.

Todd, I.A., 2004. *The Field Survey of the Vasilikos Valley* 1. Vasilikos Valley Project 9. Studies in Mediterranean Archaeology 71.9. Sävedalen, Sweden: P. Åström's Förlag.

Toth, J.A., 2002. Composite stone anchors in the ancient Mediterranean. *Acta Archaeologica Hungarica* 53: 85–118.

Valério, M., 2014. Seven uncollected Cypro-Minoan inscriptions. *Kadmos* 53: 111–127.

Valério, M., and B. Davis, 2017. Cypro-Minoan in marking systems of the eastern and central Mediterranean: new methods of investigating old questions. In A.M. Jasink, J. Weingarten and S. Ferrara (eds), *Non-scribal Communication Media in the Bronze Age Aegean and Surrounding Areas*. Periploi–Collana di Studi egei e ciprioti 9: 131–152. Florence: Firenze University Press.

van Soldt, W.H., 1989. Labels from Ugarit. *Ugarit-Forschungen* 21: 375–388.

van Soldt, W.H., 2000. Private archives at Ugarit. In A.C.V.M. Bongenaar (ed.), *Interdependency of Institutions and Private Entrepreneurs*. MOS Studies 2: 229–245. Leiden: Nederlands Historisch-Archaeologisch Instituut te Istanbul.

van Soldt, W.H., 2002. Studies on the sākinu-official (2). The function of the sākinu of Ugarit. *Ugarit-Forschungen* 34: 805–828.

van Wijngaarden, G.J., 2002. *Use and Appreciation of Mycenaean Pottery in the Levant, Cyprus and Italy*. Amsterdam: Amsterdam University Press.

Vetters, M., 2011. A clay ball with a Cypro-Minoan inscription from Tiryns. *Archäologischer Anzeiger* (2011.2): 1–49.

Vichos., Y., 1996. Point Iria wreck 1993: the stone anchors. *Enalia* 4: 17–19.

Vilain, S., 2023. Imitations, transpositions: Chypre et le Levant nord aux âges du Bronze moyen et du Bronze récent. *Syria* 100: 41–69.

Vincentelli, I., 1976. Alasia: per una storia di Cipro nell'età del Bronzo. *Studi Ciprioti e Rapporti di Scavo* 2: 9–49.

Virolleaud, C., 1940. Lettres et documents administratifs provenant des archivs d'Ugarit. *Syria* 21: 247–276.

Virolleaud, C., 1941. Textes administratifs de Ras-Shamra en cunéiforme alphabetique. *Revue d'Assyriologie* 37: 11–44.

Virolleaud, C., 1957. *Le Palais Royal d'Ugarit 2. Textes en cunéiformes alphabetiques des Archivs Est, Ouest et Centrales*. Mission de Ras Shamra 7. Paris: Klincksieck.

Virolleaud, C., 1965. *Le Palais Royal d'Ugarit* 5. Mission de Ras Shamra 11. Paris: Klincksieck.

Vita, J-P., 1999. The society of Ugarit. In W.G.E. Watson and N. Wyatt (eds), *Handbook of Ugaritic Studies*. Handbuch der Orientalistik, Abteilung 1, Der Nahe und Mittlere Osten, Band 39: 455–498. Leiden: Brill.

von Rüden, C., 2016. The ivory deposit. In C. von Rüden, A. Georgiou, A. Jacobs and P. Halstead, *Feasting, Craft and Depositional Practice in Late Bronze Age Palaepaphos. The Well Fillings of Evreti*. Bochumer Forschungen zur Ur- und Frühgeschichtlichen Archäologie 8: 291–368. Rahden-Westfallen, Germany: Verlag Marie Leidorf GmbH.

Votruba, G.F., 2019. Building upon Honor Frost's anchor-stone foundations. In L. Blue (ed.), *In the Footsteps of Honor Frost: The Life and Legacy of a Pioneer in Maritime Archaeology*, 213–244. Leiden: Sidestone Press.

Wachsmann, S., 1998. *Seagoing Ships and Seamanship in the Bronze Age Levant*. College Station: Texas A&M University Press.

Wachsmann, S., 2000. Some notes on Mediterranean seafaring during the second millennium BC. In S. Sherratt (ed.), *The Wall Paintings of Thera* 2: 803–824. Athens: Thera Foundation.

Waiman-Barak, P., T. Bürge and P.M. Fischer, 2023. Petrographic studies of Late Bronze Age pottery from Hala Sultan Tekke, Cyprus. *Journal of Archaeological Science: Reports* 49: 104038. DOI:10.1016/j.jasrep.2023.104038.

Ward, C.A., 2010. Seafaring in the Bronze Age Aegean: evidence and speculation. In D.J. Pullen (ed.), *Political Economies of the Aegean Bronze Age*, 149–160. Oxford: Oxbow.

Webb, J.M., 1999. *Ritual Architecture, Iconography and Practice in the Late Cypriote Bronze Age*. Studies in Mediterranean Archaeology and Literature, Pocketbook 75. Jonsered, Sweden: P. Åström's Förlag.

Webb, J.M., 2001. The sanctuary of the Ingot God at Enkomi: a new reading of its construction, use and abandonment. In P.M. Fischer (ed.), *Contributions to the Archaeology and History of the Bronze and Iron Ages in the Eastern Mediterranean: Studies in Honour of Paul Åström*. Österreichisches Archäologisches Institut, Sonderschriften Band 39: 69–82. Vienna: Österreichisches Archäologisches Institut.

Webb, J.M., 2002. Device, image and coercion. The role of glyptic in the political economy of Late Bronze Age Cyprus. In J. Smith (ed.), *Script and Seal Use on Cyprus in the Bronze and Iron Ages*. Archaeological Institute of America, Colloquia and Conference Papers 4: 111–154. Boston: Archaeological Institute of America.

Webb, J.M., 2018. Spatial and social discontinuities in burial practice and the privatisation of mortuary space in Bronze Age Cyprus. *Journal of Mediterranean Archaeology* 31: 203–228.

Webb, J.M., and D. Frankel, 2013. *Ambelikou Aletri: Metallurgy and Pottery Production in Middle Bronze Age Cyprus*. Studies in Mediterranean Archaeology 138. Uppsala: Åström's Förlag.

Webb, J.M., and A.B. Knapp, 2021. Rethinking Middle Bronze Age communities on Cyprus: 'egalitarian' and isolated or complex and interconnected? *Journal of Archaeological Research* 29: 203–253.

Westholm, A., 1939. Built tombs in Cyprus. *Opuscula Archaeologica* 2: 29–58.

Wright, G.R.H., 1992. *Ancient Building in Cyprus*. Handbuch der Orientalistik 7. Abteilung, Kunst und Archaeologie. Band I, Der Alte Vordere Orient, 2B/7/1 and 2B/7/2. Leiden: Brill.

Xella, P., 1981. *I Testi Rituali di Ugarit*. Studi Semitici 54. Pubblicazioni del Centro de Studio per la Civilta Fenicia e Punica 21. Rome: Consiglio Nazionale dell Ricerche.

Xenophontos, C., D. Pilides and J.C. Malpas, 2000. Petrographic analysis of Late Bronze Age pithoi from Cyprus. In D. Pilides, *Pithoi of the Late Bronze Age in Cyprus*, 169–180. Nicosia: Department of Antiquities, Cyprus.

Yamasaki, M., 2023. *Conceptualizing Bronze Age Seascapes. Concepts of the Sea and Marine Fauna in the Eastern Mediterranean in the 2nd Millennium BCE*. Studies in the Archaeology and History of the Levant and Eastern Mediterranean 2. Turhout, Belgium: Brepols.

Yoffee, N., 2014. Concluding remarks: Kanesh, the city. In L. Atici, F. Kulakoğlu, G. Barjamović and A. Fairbairn (eds), *Current Research at Kültepe-Kanesh: An Interdisciplinary and Integrative Approach to Trade Networks, Internationalism, and Identity*. Journal of Cuneiform Studies, Supplementary Series 4: 213–217.

Yon, M., 1980. Rhytons chypriotes à Ougarit. *Report of the Department of Antiquities, Cyprus*: 79–83.

Yon, M. (ed.), 1987. *Le Centre de la Ville, 38e-44e Campagne (1978-1984)*. Ras Shamra-Ougarit 3. Éditions Recherches sur les Civilisations, Mémoire 72. Paris: ADPF.

Yon, M., 1994. Ougarit et ses relations avec les régions maritimes voisines (d'après les travaux récents). In G. Brooke, A. Curtis and J. Healey (eds), *Ugarit and the Bible, Proceedings of the International Symposium on Ugarit and the Bible, Manchester, September 1992*, 421–439. Münster: Ugarit Verlag.

Yon, M., 1995. La maison d'Ourtenou dans le quartier sud d'Ougarit (fouilles 1994). *Academie des Inscriptions et Belles Lettres: Compete Rendus des Séances*: 427–451.

Yon, M., 1999a. Chypre et Ougarit à la fin du Bronze Récent. *Report of the Department of Antiquities, Cyprus*: 113–119.

Yon, M., 1999b. La Syrie et Chypre au bronze récent. In A. Caubet (ed.), *L'acrobate au taureau: les découvertes de Tel el-Dab'a (Egypte) et l'archéologie de la Méditerranée orientale (1800-1400 av. J.-C.)*, 123–148. Paris: Musée du Louvre.

Yon, M., 2000. A trading city: Ugarit and the west. *Near Eastern Archaeology* 63: 192–193.

Yon, M., 2001. White Slip in the northern Levant. In V. Karageorghis (ed.), *The White Slip Ware of Late Bronze Age Cyprus*. Österreichische Akademie der Wissenschaften, Denkschriften der Gesamtakademie 20: 117–125. Vienna: Österreichische Akademie der Wissenschaften.

Yon, M., 2003. The foreign relations of Ugarit. In N.C. Stampolidis and V. Karageorghis (eds), *Ploes.. Sea Routes…: Interconnections in the Mediterranean, 16th-6th c. BC*, 41–51. Athens: University of Crete, Leventis Foundation.

Yon, M., 2006. *The City of Ugarit at Tell Ras Shamra*. Winona Lake, Indiana: Eisenbrauns.

Yon, M., 2007. 'Au roi d'Alasia, mon père…'. *Cahier du Centre d'Études Chypriotes* 37: 15–38.

Yon, M., 2013. Cyprus et Levant nord à la fin de l'Âge du Bronze: témoignages écrits et documents archéologiques. *Pasiphae* 7: 207–219.

Yon, M., and D. Arnaud (eds), 2001. *Études Ougaritiques* I. *Travaux 1985-1995*. Ras Shamra-Ougarit 14. Paris: Éditions Recherche sur les Civilisations.

Yon, M., V. Karageorghis and N. Hirschfeld, 2000. *Céramiques mycéniennes d'Ougarit*. Ras Shamra-Ougarit 13. Paris, Nicosia: ADPF, Leventis Foundation.

Zevulun, U., 1990. Tell el-Yahudiyah juglets from a potter's refuse pit at Afula. In A. Eitan, R. Gophna and M. Kochavi (eds), *Ruth Amiran Volume*. Eretz Israel 21: 174–190. Jerusalem: Hebrew University, Israel Exploration Society.

Zukerman, A., 2012. Bronze wheeled stands in a new Ugaritic text. *Revue Biblique* 119: 481–497.

INDEX

Number in *italics* refers to a figure; number in **bold** refers to a table

A
acropolis, Ugarit   *19*, 38, 45
Aegean painted pottery   71
Aegean-type painted wares. *See* White Painted Wheelmade III ware
'Afula   52
agents, mercantile   14, 51, 66, 68, 70, 73. *See* also merchants
Alalakh   13, 61
Alašiya (Cyprus): Akkadian and Ugaritic texts mentioning   15, 34, **58–59**, 60–64, 67–68, 72, 75; king of   61, 62, 64, 72, 75, 76
Alassa   15, 16
Alassa *Paleotaverna*   27, *28*, **49**, 55
Alassa *Pano Mandilares*   **49**, 51
alṯy or *aldy* (Ugaritic: of/from Cyprus)   **58**, 60, 75
Amarna Letters   61
Ammištamru II   61–62
Ammurapi   62
Anatolia: Bichrome ware throughout southern   52; exchange activities with   23, 25, 68–69, 73; Hittite   18, 65, 74; pottery from   40, 42, 44; 'socketed axeheads' and 'warrior belts' found in   54; southern coastal   71; (coastal) western   17, 18
anchorage   26, 71. *See* also port
anchors   26, 31–32, 72, 73
Apliki *Karamallos*   26, **49**
'Apliki ware'   42
Aredhiou *Vouppes*   26, 51
Arpera *Mosphilos*   49, **49**, *50*, 53–54
ashlar masonry   15, 16, 26, 27–31, *28*, 47, 76
Ayios Iakovos *Dhima*   54–55
Ayios Iakovos *Melia*   54

B

Base-ring ware, Cypriot 15, 16, 21, **41**, 42–45, 67, 74
'bathtubs' 35
Bi'ruti 21, **58**, 64, 73
Bichrome ware 44, 52
Black Slip ware 43, 52, 53–54. *See* also Tell el-Yahudiyeh (TEY) ware
boules (clay balls), inscribed 33–34, 75
branding practices 74–76

C

Canaanite Jar (CJ): from Cyprus 49–51, **49**, *50*, 78; Levantine *21*, 67; Organic Residues Analysis on 48; provenance studies on 48, 50
cargo, maritime 15, 16, 18, **58–59**, 63–64, 67–70, 72
Centre de la ville, Ugarit 39, **41**, 43
CJ. *See* Canaanite Jar (CJ)
community: 'brand' 75, 78; coastal 71; harbour (Akkadian *kāru*) 67; mercantile 69, 77
copper: 'branded' oxhide ingots of 74–75; Cypriot resource (Troodos Ophiolite Complex) 16–18, 23–25, 32, 37, 65, 67, 69; (oxhide) ingots of 15, 16, *22*, 37; from ingot mould 23; mentioned in Akkadian and Ugaritic texts 38, **58**, **59**, 61, 63–64, 67, 69; slag at Minet el-Beidha 37
craftspeople 45, 48, 57, **58**, 60, 64
Crete 15, 18, 27–29, 32, **59**, 68
Cretan Transport Stirrup Jars (TSJs) 51, 74
Cypro-Minoan (CM) script 33–34, 36, 73, 74, 75

D

Dhali *Kafkallia* 54
dipper juglets 44, 51

E

Egypt: Bichrome ware in 52; Canaanite Jars (CJs) in 48; Cypriot copper and 65, 67; exchange relations with Cyprus 13, 25, 61; exchange relations with Ugarit 15, 23, 29, 68–69; faience vessels from 55; Levantine bronzes in 54; part of Late Bronze Age maritime sphere of interaction 18, 65, 71, 73, 74, 77; pottery from 26, 51; Tell el-Yahudiyeh (TEY) ware from 52–54
elites: Cypriot 27, 31, 43, 54–55, 78; Levantine 43, 55, 77; mercantile 55, 66–67, 68–69, 75, 76, 78; Ugarit's 38, 78
Emar **59**, 63
Enkomi: ashlar masonry at 15, 26, 27, 29, 30, 31, 47, 76; connection with Ugarit 16–18, 26, 29–31, 35–38, 42–43, 47, 55–56; cylinder seals from 36; Cypro-Minoan inscriptions of 26, 33, 75; excavations at 40, 47, 66; imported goods and specialised products at 26, 44, 47, 49, 50, 52, 54–56; ivories from 44, 55; mortuary practices at 29–31, 76; port

of   17–18, 23, 25, 26, 61, 70, 72; White Painted Wheelmade III ware
    from   42; White Slip wares from   42–43
'entrepreneurial sphere'   66–67, 76, 77
Episkopi (Kourion) *Bamboula*   25, 36

F
faience   15, 16, 25, 54–56, 69
figurines   15, 37–38, 55

G
gift: exchange   17, 74; 'greeting'   61
glass   55
gold objects   25, 54, 55–56, 72

H
Haifa Bay   48, 55
Hala Sultan Tekke: Bichrome ware   52; bowl inscribed in Ugaritic
    cuneiform   15, 55; elites engaged in workshops   75; port   17, 18, 23, 25,
    61, 70, 72; PSF3SA type anchor   32; textile manufacture at   69; White
    Painted Wheelmade   42
Hala Sultan Tekke *Vyzakia*   25, **49**, 50, 70, 76
harbour: community (Akkadian *kāru*)   67; '-master' of Ugarit   34, 36, **59**, 64,
    66–67, 68; natural   23; town   67. *See* also port
horses: burials   54, 76; exchanges of   **59**, 63, 64, 72, 73

I
imitations and 'transpositions' of Cypriot ceramics   43, 45, 55
ingot: branding of copper oxhide   74–75, 76; copper   15, 37; copper
    oxhide   16, **22**, 23, 37, 72; lead   37; mentioned in letter of Kušmešuša,
    king of *Alašiya*   **59**, 61, 69; mould of oxhide   **22**, 23, 37, 75
interaction sphere, maritime   9, 61, 70, 71–73, *71*, 78
'International Style'   55, 76
ivory: carved on Cyprus   69; connection between Cyprus and Ugarit   15,
    16–17, 35, 44, 55–56; from Enkomi   26, 35, 44, 55; Levantine imports
    on Cyprus   26, 54, 55; part of eastern Mediterranean international
    exchange system   16, 25, 69; from Ugarit   35, 39, 44; from Uluburun
    shipwreck   72; workshop   56

J
Jericho   54
jewellery   16, 26, 37, 38, 54, 56
juglet: Base-ring (I and   II)   44, 45, 74; Base-ring shaped glass   55;
    Cypriot White Painted V   30; Cypriot White Shaved   42, 44; dipper
    (*puisettes*)   44, 51; imitation of Cypriot   43, 55; Monochrome ware   45;
    Syro-Palestianian   51; Tell el-Yahudiyeh (TEY) ware   52–53; White Painted
    Wheelmade II imitation   45; White Slip   45
Jerusalem   54

K

Kalavasos *Ayios Dhimitrios*: ashlar masonry at 15, 16, 27; Canaanite Jars (CJs) from **49;** clay *boules* at 33; Building III 70, 76; Building X 16; grid system of streets 16; inscribed clay cylinders at 33; Levantine imports at 55; seals from 36; (oil production) workshops at 16, 51, 75

Kalopsidha 49, **49**, 51, 54

Karpass peninsula 25, 51

Kazaphani *Ayios Andronikos* 54

kiln, potter's ('Afula) 52

Kition: Aegean-type wares produced at 42; anchors (PSAs) at 31, 32, 72, 73; ashlar masonry at 15, 27; Canaanite Jars (CJs) at **49**; elites from 75; grid system of streets at 16; Levantine imports at 51, 55; parallels between metal figurines from Ugarit and 37–38; port 17, 18, 23, 61, 70, 72, 76; sailing time from Sidon to 26; 'Temple' 1 at 70

Kition *Bamboula* 15, **49**, 51

Kition *Chrysopolitissa* 55

Klavdhia *Trimithios* 54

Kom Rabia (Memphis, Egypt) 48

Kommos 32

Kouklia *Evreti* **49**, 56

Kouklia *Palaepaphos* 25, **49**. *See also* *Palaepaphos*

Kültepe 54

kupirijo goods 74

Kušmešuša, king of *Alašiya* **59**, 61, 69, 72

L

Lapithos 51, 54

luxury items: Cypriot 16, Levantine 16, 54, 55–56, 78, on Uluburun shipwreck 72

M

Ma'ḫadu. *See* Minet al-Beidha (Ma'ḫadu)

Maa *Palaeokastro* 49, **49**, 50, 70, *70*, 76

Maison au Sud du Temple aux Rhytons, Ugarit 39, **41**, 43

Maison du Grand-Prêtre, Ugarit 35, 38

Maritime Transport Container (MTC) 48, 51, 72. *See also* Canaanite Jar (CJ); (Cretan) Transport Stirrup Jar (TSJ)

Maroni 17, 26, 27, 61, 70

Maroni *Tsaroukkas* 70, 76

Maroni *Vournes* 16, **49**, 51

Megiddo 30, 55

merchants: Aegean 28; branding or marking of goods by 51, 74–75; Cypriot 16, 54, 65, 66, 67, 69–70; Cypriot, based at Ugarit 28, 64, 72, 76; Cyprus and Bronze Age 17–18, 25, 69; consumption practices of 51, 78; familial relationship between 31, 72, 76, 77, 78; foreign 66–70, 73, 77; as intermediaries 43–44, 51; Levantine 32, 67, 69, 76; of Minet el-Beidha 67; origin of 71–74, 75; relationship of king of Ugarit with 23,

66, 68, 73; of Ugarit, based at Enkomi   26; of Ugarit   13, 29, **58–59**, 60, 64–69, 72–73, 76–78. *See* also traders

merchants' houses   23, 36, 69, 70, *70*. *See* also House of Rap'ānu; House of Rašap-Abu; House of Urtenu; House of Yabninu

Mesopotamia, northern   23, 69

Minet el-Beidha (Ma'ḥadu): anchors at   32, 73; ashlar masonry at   28–29; Canaanite Jars (CJs) at   *21*, 21; cylinder seals at   36; Cypriot imports at   21, 40, **41**, 43–46, 69, 78; metallic material at   37; Mycenaean wares at   45; port of Ugarit   17, *20*, 21, 29, 32, 66–67; possible merchant warehouses   67; tombs at   21, 28–30, 35, 39, 40, **41**, 43–45

mkrm (Sumerian DAM.GÀR, merchants)   **58**, 66, 68, 72–73, 76–78. *See* also *tamkāru* (Akkadian)

Monochrome wares   43, 45

Morphou *Toumba tou Skourou*   25, 53–54

mortuary practices   25, 26, 29–31

MTC. *See* Maritime Transport Container (MTC)

Mycenaean ware   15, 43–44, 45–46

Myrtou *Pigadhes*   16, **49**

N

network analysis   18

network: exchange   25, 65, 77, 78; closed exchange   74; mercantile (maritime)   67, 69–70, 75, 77; open exchange   85; Ugarit as locus of Cypriot distribution   76

Nicosia *Ayia Paraskevi*   51, 54

Niqmaddu III, king of Ugarit   **59**, 61, 62, 64, 69, 72

Nitovikla Fortress   27, **49**, 52

O

olive oil   16, 45, 48, 63, 73

ostrich eggs   54, 72

oxhide ingot: copper   16, *22*, 23, 37, 72, 74, 75; mould   22, 37, 75

P

Palaepaphos   15, 25

'pierced stone' (PSA) anchor   32, 73

'planar stone-frame staked' anchor, PSF3SA-type   32, 73

pithos: Cypriot   74, 78; from House of Yabninu   40; from Kition   51; from Pyla *Kokkinokremos*   51; rim inscribed with Cypro-Minoan from House of Urtenu   33

Plain wares, Levantine   51

Plain White ware   **41**, 44

Point Iria shipwreck   32

Politiko *Chomazoudhia*   54

Politiko *Phorades*   26

port: of 'Atlg   64; of Cyprus   17–18, 25, 44, 69–70, 72, 77, 78; eastern Mediterranean   17, 71; Enkomi   17–18, 23, 25, 26, 70, 72; Episkopi (Kourion) *Bamboula*   25; facilities   73; Hala Sultan Tekke   17, 18, 23, 70, 72, 76; Hala Sultan Tekke *Vyzakia*   25, 70; Kalavasos *Ayios Dhimitrios*   70, 76; Kition   17, 18, 23, 70, 72, 76; Levantine   69, 77; Maa *Palaeokastro*   70, 76; Maroni *Tsaroukkas*   17, 26, 70, 76; Minet el-Beidha (Ma'ḫadu)   17, 21, 29, 32, 46, 66–67; Morphou *Toumba tou Skourou*   25; origin of (wrecked) ships   31, 71; Ras el-Bassit   19; Ras Ibn Hani   16, 21–22, 29, 46, 66, 75; Tel Abu Hawam   72; of Ugarit   21, 40, 48, 72, 77. *See* also anchorage; harbour

potmarks and potter's marks   74–75

Pyla *Kokkinokremos*   13, 33, 49, **49**, 50, 51, 55

R

rābiṣu ('senior prefect')   **59**, 61, 62–63

Rap'ānu: House of   *19*, 34, 66, 75; merchant   23, 36, 66, 68, 76

Ras el-Bassit   19

Ras ibn Hani: Cypriot pottery at   40, 45, 78; grid system of streets   16; imitations and 'transpositions' of Cypriot ceramics at   45; major recipient of copper and tin   67; maybe ancient *Bi'ruti*, *Appu* or *Ra'šu*   21, **58**, **59**, 62, 64, 73; metallurgical installations at   22, 37; Mycenaean ware at   45–46; oxhide ingot mould at   22, 37, 75; port of Ugarit   16, 21–22, 29, 46, 66, 75; textual evidence from   22, **58**, **59**, 62, 66; use of stone-cut masonry at   29

Rašap-Abu: harbour-master   23, 34, 66, 66–67, 68; House of   *19*, 34, 36, **59**, 66, 75, 76

Red and Black Burnished wares, Syrian   51

Red Lustrous ware   **41**, 42, 44, 45

Red Slip ware, Cypriot   42, 43

Red-on-Black ware   **41**, 42, 43

rhyton   15, 42, 55

royal palace: Ras Ibn Hani ('South Palace')   22; Ugarit   18, *19*, 29, 35, 37, **41**, 43, 64, 76

Rude or Pastoral Style ceramics. *See* White Painted Wheelmade III ware

S

sākinu ('prefect')   **59**, 64, 68, 75

Sanidha *Moutti tou Ayiou Serkou*   26

'sea peoples' 62. *See* also Šikila

seal: Cypriot, at Ugarit   35, 36, 75; cylinder   26, 36, 54, 64, 72; iconography of   36, 64, 72, 78; from tomb at House of Rap'ānu   36; stone   16, 36; use of seal   68, 75

seal impressions: Cypriot   33, 34, 35, 36; Cypro-Minoan inscribed   33, 36 ships: builders, investors and owners of   23, 65, 68, 72–73, 76, 77; cargo of   15, 16, 18, **58–59**, 63–64, 67–70, 72; commercial sailing   77; Cypriot   18, 31, 66, 69, 72; Levantine   31, 72; merchants living on   67; models   77; origin of   31, 32, 71, 72, 73–75; 'people who live on' (*Šikila*)   **59**, 62–63, 73; perishable materials on   56; for regional and interregional trade   72; in Ugaritic and Akkadian texts   23, 55, **58–59**, 62–64, 66, 68, 72–73

shipwreck: Cape Gelidonya   33; Hishuley Carmel   33; Point Iria   32; port of origin of   31; Uluburun   17, 48, 72, 74–75

Sidon   26, 48, 53

Šikila (people 'who live on ships'; 'sea peoples')   **59**, 62–63, 73

silver: inscribed bowl   33, 38, 55; payments in   68; at Ugarit   37; from Uluburun shipwreck   72

Sinaranu, merchant from Ugarit   59, 68, 72

Siyannu kingdom   19

spheres of interaction, maritime   9, 61, 70, 71–73, *71*, 78

spindle bottles   42

spindle whorls   35, 35

stands, bronze wheeled   38

stirrup jars   15, 74. *See* also (Cretan) Transport Stirrup Jars (TSJs)

'Style Rude Chypro-Mycenien'. *See* White Painted Wheelmade III ware

šulmanu, a royal 'greeting gift'   61

T

tamkāru (Akkadian, merchant)   66, 67, 68. *See* also *mkrm* (Sumerian DAM.GÀR, merchants)

Tel Abu Hawam   48, 72

Tel Dan   30

Tel Kabri   53

Tell Arqa   48

Tell ed-Dab'a   52, 53, 54

Tell el-Far'ah North   54

Tell el-Yahudiyeh (TEY) ware   52–54

Tell Kazel   45, 48

Tell Tweini   30

textiles   25, 64, 69, 72

TEY ware. *See* Tell el-Yahudiyeh (TEY) ware

timber and wood   16, 25, 48, 63, 69

tin   18, 38, **58**, 64, 67, 72

Tochni *Lakkia*   26

tombs: Arpera *Mosphilos* 49, 53; ashlar 28–29, 30, 76; Enkomi 27, 29–31, 35, 47, 55, 76; at House of Rap'ānu 36; Kalopsidha 54; Kition 55; Kition *Chrysopolitissa* 55; Lapithos 54; MC III-LC I tombs 49; Megiddo 30; Minet el-Beidha 21, 28–30, 35, 39, 40, **41**, 43–45; Morphou *Toumba tou Skourou* 53; pit or shaft 30; Politiko *Chomazoudhia* 54; Ras Ibn Hani 22; Tel Dan 30; Tell Tweini 30; *tholos*-type 30, 31; *tholos*-type with beehive shaped superstructure 30; Ugarit (Ras Shamra) 28–31, 39, 40, **41**, 43, 45, 76

trade: agreements 73; cabotage 17; between Cyprus and Ugarit 78; of Cyprus with the Levant and Egypt 13; emporium 73, 78; long-distance 17, 71–72, 74; mechanisms 74; metal 67, 76; networks of international 69; relations 54; seaborne 17, 25, 26, 65, 69, 71–72, 77; Ugarit's maritime 66–68, 73, 75–76, 78; in Ugaritic and Akkadian texts **58–59**, 65, 67

traders 17, 23, 36, 65, 67–68, 75, 77. *See* also merchants

Transport Stirrup Jars (TSJs) 51, 74. *See* also stirrup jars

tripods and stands, bronze 15, 38, 69

Troodos mountains 23, 62, 63

TSJs. *See* (Cretan) Transport Stirrup Jars

Tudḫaliya IV **59**, 62

U

Uluburun shipwreck 17, 48, 72, 74–75

Urtenu, House of: Cypriot wares at 43, 66; elite merchant 66, 68, 76; 'labels' and objects inscribed with Cypro-Minoan at 23, 33, 36, 66; mentioned in tablet from royal palace 64; plan *19*; seal impressions from 36; texts from 15, 19, 23, **58–59**, 60, 62–63, 68, 75

W

wall bracket, Cypriot **41**, 44

warrior burials 54, 76

weights 16, 37, 39, 54

weight standards 61

White Painted Pendent Line Style 42, 43, 44

White Painted ware 15, 30, **41**, 42, 43

White Painted Wheelmade II juglet 45

White Painted Wheelmade III ware (*also* Rude or Pastoral Style ceramics; 'Style Rude Chypro-Mycenien') **41**, 42, 43–44

White Shaved ware 15, 21, **41**, 42, 43, 44

White Slip ware: at Enkomi 42; at Minet el-Beidha and Ugarit 15, 21, **41**, 42–45, 69; imitations and 'transpositions' of 45; lead isotope analysis on 44; Neutron Activation Analysis (NAA) on 42; Proto- 42; technically improved hemispheric bowls of 69

wine: in Canaanite Jars (CJs) 48, 49; (Cypriot) ships carrying 18, 69, 73; Ugaritic text mentioning provision of ration of 57, **58**, 60, 72–73; workshop for producing and deposit of 67 wood and timber   16, 25, 48, 63, 69

workshop: *boules* as 'identity card' of individuals engaged in   75; Cypriot   40, 42, 75; ivory   56; metal   37, 56; oil production   16, 51, 67; wine production   67; Tell el-Yahudiyeh (TEY) ware   53

Y

Yabninu, House of: Cypro-Minoan tablets from   34, 66; elite merchant   23, 66, 68, 76; operated (semi-)independently   73; plan   *19*; publication of excavation of   40; Ugaritic and Akkadian texts from   66